NEWS FOR A CHANGE

An Advocate's Guide to Working With the Media

Lawrence Wallack • Katie Woodruff • Lori Dorfman • Iris Diaz

SAGE Publications
International Educational and Professional Publisher
Thousand Oaks   London   New Delhi

For information:

SAGE Publications, Inc.
2455 Teller Road
Thousand Oaks, California 91320
E-mail: order@sagepub.com

SAGE Publications Ltd.
6 Bonhill Street
London EC2A 4PU
United Kingdom

SAGE Publications India Pvt. Ltd.
M-32 Market
Greater Kailash I
New Delhi 110 048 India

Printed in the United States of America

Library of Congress Cataloging-in-Publication Data

Main entry under title:

News for a change: An advocate's guide to working with the media /
by Lawrence Wallack . . . [et al.].
    p. cm.
  Includes bibliographical references (p.   ) and index.
  ISBN 978-0-7619-1923-0 (cloth : alk. paper)
  ISBN 978-0-7619-1924-7 (pbk : alk. paper)
  1. Press and politics—United States. 2. Press and
propaganda—United States. 3. Advocacy advertising—United States.
4. Social advocacy—United States. 5. United States—Politics and
government—1993- . I. Wallack, Lawrence Marshall.
  PN4888.P6 N48 1999
  070.4'49324'0973—dc21   99-6310

07 08 09 10 9 8

Acquiring Editor:	Margaret H. Seawell
Editorial Assistant:	Renée Piernot
Production Editor:	Diana E. Axelsen
Editorial Assistant:	Karen Wiley
Typesetter/Designer:	Janelle LeMaster
Indexer:	Virgil Diodato
Cover Designer:	Candice Harman

CONTENTS

FOREWORD

I remember getting a frantic call some five years ago. It was from a young public health advocate desperately trying to figure out how to "get media" for a policy initiative that would launch in five days. She said she heard of this thing called media advocacy, and she wanted me to explain how to do it—in 10 minutes. After that, she had to pick up her son from day care.

I think I spent the first five minutes laughing. Then, I tried to help her as best as I could. Mostly, I wished there was some easy-to-use book that would give her what she needed to know when she needed it.

Well, you are holding that book right now

Actually, this is more of a guide than a book. The words speak plainly, the examples are accessible, and the exercises will make you a genuine media maven before you know it. This is not another academic explication of why media are important; anybody who has finally admitted that a computer is better than a typewriter has got that one figured out. This is a guide for people who want to make a difference and know media can help them get there.

This book is about how media coverage affects the political context that shapes social change efforts and how you can put its power to work for you. Once you read it, you will never again feel comfortable just handing out brochures (no matter how cool they are) or hosting yet another seminar. Once you "get" media advocacy, you have to do it. Or live with the fact that you're not doing everything you can to make a difference.

There's plenty of evidence that media advocacy works. In tobacco reporting, the media's shift from the smoker to the industry is one of the more potent examples. Advances in gun control, AIDS research, and alcohol policy offer more evidence. In each case, organizations started with clear policy objectives and desired outcomes and then figured out how media could advance their goals. And the results are impressive.

Who would've thought (even five years ago) that the tobacco industry, under siege of litigation, would be forced to consider a major settlement? Alcohol advertising and billboards no longer beckon children on their way to school in many communities, and the National Rifle Association no longer dominates the public conversation on gun control. Not perfect victories, but victories nonetheless—and none of them would have happened without effective, grassroots media advocacy.

The folks who wrote this book eat, drink, and sleep this stuff. They are activists in academicians' clothing, who were a part of these victories and many others on the public health front. They work with communities in the trenches to help them tell their stories—and tell them well.

This book is chock-full of those stories. What went right and, perhaps more important, what went wrong. There's also plenty of advice from activists in their own words as well as some of their best sound bites, all waiting to be, well . . . uh . . . appropriated. It's like 20 years of hard-earned experience right in your hands.

The high science of media advocacy is here, too. And I do mean science because under similar conditions, you can replicate these results. This book elegantly summarizes this knowledge, from message development techniques to that all important media effects research on what works and why. After so many years of observation, the authors have definitely isolated the lessons and laid them out brilliantly here. Soon, you too will understand why tear-jerking, personal stories can be downright harmful in this work; and you may think twice about that cute photo opportunity at the local preschool. Building support and influencing others require that we pay attention to images and make them work on our behalf. This book will help you apply this science in practical, down-to-earth ways.

We have stories to tell: vital stories, stories that could help save lives if only we could garner the attention and the political will. This book will make the job a whole lot easier.

Don't wait until the last minute to get the expert media guidance you need. Just turn the page and begin right here, right now.

—Makani Themba-Nixon
Director, Grassroots Innovative Policy Program
Applied Research Center
Oakland, California

PREFACE

A while ago, I was completing a presentation on media advocacy when some-one from the audience asked, "But if we get a lot of attention in the media, won't it just mobilize the opposition?" I was very surprised. The question seemed to suggest that remaining invisible was a desirable strategy. I realized that it wasn't the first time I had heard this question, although this was the clearest that it had ever been stated. It seems that for some advocates, being invisible and not drawing attention to their issue is seen as a kind of strategy; they avoid controversy and make only tentative requests for change.

Many others, however, know that power and visibility are important to amplify concerns and advance effective approaches. They know that reticence and invisibility are the problem, not the solution.

Frederick Douglass, the 19th-century African American abolitionist, said, "Power concedes nothing without a demand." Daniel Schorr, the 20th-century journalist, said, "If you don't exist in the media, you don't exist." The lesson is that advocates need both visibility and power. Strategic media approaches can help deliver the visibility necessary to enhance power in this media-driven age. Media advocacy is one such strategy: It is the strategic use of news media and, when appropriate, paid advertising, to support community organizing to advance a public policy initiative. It gives visibility to and "certifies" the existence of those demanding change. It adds an exclamation point to the demand.

The emergence and spread of media advocacy over the last decade has been fueled by a growing frustration among progressive groups who feel their voices have not been heard and their issues not seen. At the same time, it reflects an increasing sophistication about how social change happens. Rather than cursing the news media, or complaining about their indifference or outright hostility, people are now trying to harness the power of the media to advance their social policy goals.

Some argue that the emergence of media savvy among community groups is a worrisome development that signifies surrender to the enemy. By conforming to the myth that our complex issues can be boiled down to media bites of 8 to 12 seconds, it is felt that we have, in effect, given up and tacitly agreed to trivialize our issues. There is something to be said for this perspective, which argues that the real problem is news media that trivialize issues by communicating in a shallow, often sensationalistic manner with no attention to the broader social, economic, and political context. In fact, many individuals and organizations are working to make news media more representative, substantive, and responsive, and these are important efforts.

But in the meantime, despite its limitations, the news is far too powerful a force to be ignored. Unless we use our creativity and commitment to participate in the public debate, our perspectives will be left out. Our diverse voices will not be heard, and our faces not seen. Our issues will be shaped by others, and our goals will remain a private dream harbored by a select few rather than a coherent vision that can be understood and shared by others. Participating in shaping the public debate on our issues is essential. Understanding and working through the news media to promote social change is a method of refining that participation and helping to ensure that our particular story gets told the way we intend.

The tone and material in this book assume that the authors and readers are united on the socially progressive side of a range of important public issues. Often during media advocacy training, someone will ask with great concern whether the "other side" couldn't use these strategies for less "noble" goals. Well, not only *could* they use them but they *are* using them. Since the mid-1970s, conservative think tanks have excelled in setting the public agenda and framing the debate on critical issues; the consequences have been significant and damaging on a range of progressive concerns. Gregg Easterbrook noted that conservative think tanks such as the Heritage Foundation have "transformed the terms of the public policy debate,"[1] and media strategies have been central to their success.

To take just one example, look at affirmative action, a social program long supported by both major political parties and by the general public. This program, a modest effort at advancing a more just society, has recently been reframed as "preferences for people of color" and "reverse discrimination" against white males. This reframing has been so complete that news organizations routinely use the terms *preferences* and *affirmative action* interchangeably as if they are the same thing—despite the fact that pollsters consistently find that support for affirmative action is much higher than for preferences. Thus, the control of the language is critical—and progressives have to become as savvy as the right in shaping the language and effectively getting it into the public debate on social issues.

Muriel Rukeyser said, "The world is made up of stories, not atoms." There is nothing so compelling as a good story. Stories provide lessons, point directions, reflect and reinforce values, and provide a soul for bloodless concepts and ideas. Communication is about being a good storyteller, and mass communication is about telling the story in ways that take full advantage of the medium. Our side has great stories, great values, and great hopes. Unless we can better link these stories with policies and constituencies, and effectively convey them through the news media to create change, our hopes will remain only hopes. This book is designed to help make that critical link.

Lawrence Wallack
Berkeley, California

Note

1. Easterbrook, G. (1986, January). "Ideas Move Nations," *The Atlantic Monthly, 257*(1), 66-80.

———————◆•———————

The press is no substitute for institutions. It is like the beam of a searchlight that moves restlessly about, bringing one episode and then another out of darkness into vision. Men cannot do the work of the world by this light alone. They cannot govern society by episodes, incidents, and eruptions. It is only when they work by a steady light of their own that the press, when it is turned about them, reveals a situation intelligible enough for a popular decision.

Walter Lippmann, Public Opinion, *1922*

———————◆•———————

ACKNOWLEDGMENTS

Thanks to the many dedicated people who are working in many different ways to make the world better. Among those whose stories and insights have informed this book are: Hilary Abramson, Frank Acosta, Leah Aldridge, Lisa Aliferis, Michael Balooing, Dan Beauchamp, Brenda Bell-Caffee, Fran Biderman, Charlie Blek, Mary Leigh Blek, James Brennan, Margaret Brodkin, Deane Calhoun, Herb Chao-Gunther, Vivian Chavez, Mark Chekal, Hunter Cutting, Susan DeFrancesco, Kim Deterline, Kate Ertz-Berger, Gina Glantz, Eric Gorovitz, Anne Guthrie, George Hacker, Bobby Heard, Karen Hughes, Shanto Iyengar, David Jernigan, Jerome Karabel, Joan Kiley, Ethel Klein, Becca Knox, Lisa Lederer, Laurie Leiber, Judy Lipshutz, Jennifer Logan, Dan Macallair, Andrew McGuire, Kae McGuire, Elizabeth McLoughlin, Adina Medina, Marcia Meyer, Jim Mosher, Miriam Navarro-Thoms, Ellin O'Leary, Mark Pertschuk, Mike Pertschuk, Judy Pope, Holly Potter, Rene Redwood, Michael Rodriguez, Janice Rogers, Bernardo Rosa, Don Ryan, Vincent Schiraldi, Richard Scribner, Randy Shaw, Jim Shultz, Suzi Shupe, Michael Siegel, Andres Soto, Sherman Spears, Makani Themba-Nixon, Kimberly Thomas, Luis Vergara, Billie Weiss, Phil Wilbur, Katressa Williams, Garen Wintemute, Maureen Woodson, Rose Works, Pat Wright, and Elva Yañez.

We are grateful to Tony Chen, Jennifer Elias, Linda Nettekoven, Jane Ellen Stevens, Elaine Villamin, and Phil Wilbur for their helpful comments on drafts of the manuscript.

Thanks to the Berkeley Media Studies Group team for their support: Rosemary Cole, Valerie Fuller, Aixa Gannon, Elaine Villamin, and Liana Winett.

We thank Makani Themba-Nixon for the X brand cigarettes case study and "Key Questions in Choosing a Target" in Chapter 1.

We thank Kim Deterline and Hunter Cutting for many of the "Components of a Successful Media Bite" in Chapter 4.

We thank Jennifer Elias for "Paid Media: Tips for Success" and "How to Create and Place an Ad" in Chapter 8.

Earlier versions of sections of Chapters 3 and 4 first appeared in the series "Blowing Away the Smoke," media advocacy advisories for tobacco control advocates, published by the Advocacy Institute, Washington, D.C.

Development of this book was partially supported by a grant to the Berkeley Media Studies Group from the W. K. Kellogg Foundation. The authors particularly thank Tom Reis of the Kellogg Foundation for his commitment to supporting communications that address public health issues and his belief in the value of this project.

The book also reflects experiences gained on other projects funded by the Alliance to End Childhood Lead Poisoning, Americans for a Fair Chance, the California Endowment, the California Wellness Foundation, the David and Lucile Packard Foundation, and the Miriam and Peter Haas Fund.

INTRODUCTION

The person who says it cannot be done should get out of the way of the person doing it.

Chinese Proverb

When Susan DeFrancesco heard that 9-year-old Jillian Richey had been crushed to death by a collapsing slide at a suburban Pittsburgh playground, she knew that it was no accident. DeFrancesco, a lawyer with a background in injury control, had founded Injury Prevention Works, a small nonprofit organization that acted as a clearinghouse for information on playground safety and advocated for the interests of children. She had been working with the Health and Safety Committee of the Pennsylvania State PTA on making playgrounds safer. A key state legislator whose son had also been injured on a playground was ready to introduce legislation to improve playground safety statewide.

Now the death of 9-year-old Jillian put the media spotlight on this issue; DeFrancesco wanted to focus that light to raise community awareness and bring about policy change to prevent further tragedies on Pittsburgh playgrounds. That Jillian's grief-stricken father had said on the news that the tragedy was a "freak accident" was an added impetus for DeFrancesco to get to the media and make sure that people realized that injuries are not accidents. Sensible planning and adherence to basic design standards, not luck, were the requirements for safe playgrounds. And DeFrancesco had the expertise to make key people understand this important distinction.

The tragedy put the media spotlight on this issue; DeFrancesco wanted to focus that light to emphasize the policy approaches that would prevent further tragedies.

In the days following the death, DeFrancesco met with several reporters at local playgrounds to discuss the incident; she brought her own daughter to provide a visual of a child playing on the equipment. DeFrancesco consistently emphasized two points: (a) the event was not a freak accident and (b) it could have been prevented. For a year prior to the tragedy, she had worked with a city council member to develop local legislation mandating a safety review and upgrade of the city's playgrounds. The legislation was ready to be introduced, and supporters were able to draw on the community's current interest in the safety issue.

DeFrancesco wrote a letter to the editor of the local newspaper to let the community know about the city's upcoming public hearing on the playground safety legislation and to tell people how to make arrangements to testify. Mr. Richey, the father of the child who had died, attended the council hearing. His 30-second plea to the Council—"Please don't let my daughter die in vain; this accident could have been prevented"—was highlighted by the media covering the hearing. His own view of his daughter's death had been changed, presumably by his exposure to injury prevention messages in the local media.

The ordinance to assess, plan for, and upgrade the city's playgrounds passed 6 to 0 with two abstentions. In addition to the Pittsburgh ordinance, a playground in suburban Edgewood was renovated through the efforts of a local residents' group. Although the bill to mandate the improvement of playgrounds across the state did not pass, progress was made: With the help of other concerned citizens and effective media strategies, DeFrancesco achieved some success and helped prevent future injuries.

Outrage to Action

We tell DeFrancesco's story here to show how using media strategically can help advance your goals, no matter what issue you work on. There is a wonderful bumper sticker that says, "If you are not outraged, you are not paying attention." These days, many different issues enrage people: violence, lack of affordable housing, campaign finance abuses, racism, handguns, alcohol, HIV/AIDS, even cutbacks in operating hours of local libraries. Some people channel their anger into constructive action; others just get depressed or alienated, feeling their voices cannot be heard.

The energy generated by outrage or concern *can* be transformed into action for change. This book can help you do exactly that by increasing your knowledge and skills to better work through the news media to become a building block for hope and, ultimately, social change.

This is a handbook for developing a strategy that combines key elements of social change—community organizing, research, policy development, advocacy, and politics—with news media. The purpose of the strategy is to amplify your concern into a collective voice that helps to shape the media agenda and ultimately the policy agenda. The process is guided by a blend of advocacy and strategic thinking that comes before any media work.

Outrage alone will only take you so far; then, you need a plan for moving ahead and an assortment of tools to put the plan into action. So this book offers ideas on developing a practical solution to the problems you want to confront and an overall strategy for making it happen. If you know your problem, have a practical, concrete policy approach to advance, and have a good sense of the social, political, and economic context of your issue, advancing your case through the news media can dramatically increase your effectiveness.

Why Use Media?

Many organizations simply feel that they do not have the time to incorporate media into their overall social change strategy. If necessary, they might react to news stories or, sometimes, they might call a journalist with a story idea. But for the most part, they just have too many other important things to do to put in the time necessary to use media as an advocacy tool.

However, we feel strongly that every organization with a goal of social change should have a strategy for effectively putting the power of the news media to work. Before we get into the *how* of developing media strategies, we want to devote some brief attention to *why* you should concern yourself with the media. Clearly, you already know media approaches are important, or you wouldn't be reading this book. But you may need some information to convince others in your organization to devote energy and resources to media work, or you may want to know more about what research has shown about the effect of media on public opinion and social change.

The media can provide visibility, legitimacy, and credibility to an issue and to the organization advocating for change. By selecting some events and not others for news coverage, the media send a signal to the public about what is important and worth thinking about. The media also provide advocates with an avenue to reach those people whose power can help move the issue on the policy agenda. Put simply, the news media communicate to opinion leaders and influential people, as well as the general public, what issues they should think about, how they should think about them, and who has worthwhile things to say about the issues.

> *Every organization with a goal of social change should have a strategy for effectively putting the power of the news media to work.*

Talking to Power

Advocates need to reach the people who can change the rules and regulations by which our society is organized. These rules and regulations ultimately allocate the risks and benefits across society; advocates often need to change the rules as a way to reallocate risks and benefits in a more just manner. For this reason, opinion leaders, policymakers, corporate executives, and other influential people are often primary targets of advocacy efforts.

For various reasons, advocates often cannot speak directly or effectively to these people: Maybe they don't return phone calls, or maybe they make promises in private meetings but then do not deliver. Media can be a powerful tool in opening that private conversation up to the entire community and speaking to decision makers. Seeing the issue covered in the news may make decision makers feel that the entire community is in on the conversation and expecting them to act.

The Agenda-Setting Process and Reality

The world is full of problems and stories, but only some of them ever come to public attention. Certainly, many of the problems not covered in the news are important; they may even be more important than those that are covered. However, in the intense competition for media attention, few issues manage to win space.

James Dearing and Everett Rogers explain, "The agenda-setting process is an ongoing competition among issue proponents to gain the attention of media professionals, the public, and policy elites."[1] Thus, the agenda-setting process involves the media agenda, the public agenda, and the policy agenda.

Research provides good evidence that the media set the public agenda: The more an issue is covered in the news, the more likely it is to be an issue of concern to the public, as measured through public opinion polls. Oddly enough, "real world indicators"—good old reality—have much less of an impact on public opinion than the media agenda does.[2] For instance, even though crime rates have declined dramatically in many cities over recent years, crime still attracts extensive media coverage and, accordingly, remains high on the public's agenda—that is, people still fear being victimized, despite real-world risk having dropped dramatically. In a *Los Angeles Times* poll, 80% of respondents said the media's coverage of violent crime had increased their personal fear of being a victim[3]—despite the decline in real-world violence.

News is more than just a reflection of actual events; indeed, news has a powerful influence on people's perceptions of the world. News media portrayals, rather than reflecting reality, become reality.

Shaping the Debate

In 1963, Bernard Cohen provided the basis for the agenda-setting concept when he explained that the press "may not be successful much of the time in telling people what to think, but it is stunningly successful much of the time in telling people what to think about."[4] However, recent research from the field of political science provides important new insights into this old observation. The findings suggest that the way that the news media present the issue also shapes how people think about the issue.

Researcher Shanto Iyengar looked at the relationship between how television news stories are shaped and the effect of these news stories on how the audience thinks about the problem. Iyengar's work illustrates that the most typical TV news format presents news reports in terms of individual stories and isolated events. Crime, for example, might be covered from the perspective of a victim; a health story might present the experience of someone fighting a terrible disease. This kind of news story tends to be concrete, specific, personal, and visual. These are personal stories that effectively engage us and draw us in. About 80% of television network news consists of such episodic reports.[5]

The remaining 20% of news is composed of thematic stories, which are quite different. These stories tend to focus more on the context of the problem. Although thematic reports may still contain individual stories, they also include "talking heads" and charts, as well as more information about broader social forces that contribute to the issue.

The problem with typical news coverage, Iyengar found, is that when people see episodic news stories and then are asked what should be done about the problem covered in the story, their response tends to be that the person with the problem should work harder to fix it. After viewing thematic reports, however, viewers are more likely to hold government, business, and other institutions accountable as well as individuals.

For instance, viewers who see episodic stories on poverty tend to blame poor people for the problem, saying they choose this lifestyle or could try harder to find work. On the other hand, viewers who are shown thematic stories on the issue tend to blame public officials, government budget cuts, and corporate changes, such as the transfer of jobs overseas, for the problem of poverty. The difference is between reinforcing a "blaming the victim" perspective and focusing on shared responsibility and social accountability.

The disturbing implication of Iyengar's research is that stories that tend to be the most compelling, most interesting, and most engaging to the most people may have the effect of diverting attention away from the social and political causes of and solutions for problems. The very characteristics that make for a good news story are the same ones that detract from the message progressive advocates are trying to convey. Even when the story is one that many social agencies might believe to be wonderful coverage—a family is shown overcoming obstacles related to poverty through the helpful hand of a social program—the message the audience may be getting is that individual initiative is the key and as long as people try hard enough, they can succeed without outside help.

This research shows how important news is in shaping perceptions of the social problems you want to address. Advocates should not be discouraged by these challenges but rather commit themselves to participate in the public debate and try to shape emerging thematic stories that will advance positive policy outcomes. The rest of this handbook is designed to help you do just that.

The very characteristics that make for a good news story are the same ones that detract from the message progressive advocates are trying to convey.

What You Can Expect From This Handbook

We've designed this book around 10 key rules that should shape your media efforts. Throughout each chapter, we provide *Advocacy in Action* examples— stories of groups who have used media successfully to advance their policy goals—as well as checklists, pointers, worksheets, and exercises to help you apply the lessons of media advocacy to your work. Additional resources are collected in appendices at the end of the book.

No book can cover everything there is to know about working with the media. But we hope this book will help you in three key areas.

- First, this handbook will help you "pay attention" to the news media. We are often amazed by how many groups with a social change agenda do not have the time, interest, or desire to understand the importance of the media as a strategic resource. In our society, as we have seen, the media not only tell people what issues to think about but also shape how people think about those issues. Those who oppose your goals will not ignore the power of the news media, you can be sure of that—and you cannot afford to ignore it, either.

- Second, this handbook will help you integrate a media strategy into an overall strategy. The news media and paid advertising should *support* organizing and policy development activities, not replace them. Although this handbook is about media, it really has more to do with strategic thinking—shaping your argument and advancing it in ways that will increase the likelihood of achieving social change.

- Third, this handbook will help you become more comfortable participating in the public debate through the news media. You will gain the confidence and skills to call journalists, pitch stories, answer hard questions, write letters to the editor and op-ed pieces, design news events, and make interviews work for you. This handbook will increase your sophistication in working with the news media and make you and your group more effective.

What this handbook does *not* do is provide any guarantees that you will achieve your desired policy outcome. No book could make such a promise. What we do promise, however, is that you will be better able to participate in the public debate about your issue and be more effective in getting your story told. We are confident about this because we work with and have observed so many others who provide continuing proof that savvy media approaches can further the goal of social change. We will tell some of their stories in these pages and show you exactly how to ask the tough questions and do the preparation to make media work for you, too.

Notes

1. Dearing, J., & Rogers, E. (1996). *Agenda-setting.* Thousand Oaks, CA: Sage, p. 27.

2. Dearing & Rogers, 1996.

3. Braxton, G. (1997, June 4). Ratings vs. crime rates. *Los Angeles Times,* p. B1.

4. Cohen, B. (1963). *The press and foreign policy.* Princeton, NJ: Princeton University Press, p. 13.

5. Iyengar, S. (1991). *Is anyone responsible? How television frames political issues.* Chicago: University of Chicago Press.

1

DEVELOPING STRATEGY

---◆·---

Never doubt that a small group of thoughtful committed citizens can change the world; indeed, it's the only thing that ever has.

Anthropologist Margaret Mead

---◆·---

Changing the world, or just your own community, is a difficult task, and you must bring all available resources to bear on the challenge. The news media are one of the most valuable and powerful resources for change in our society—yet they are also very misunderstood and poorly used. Effectively integrating media strategies into social change efforts can be the difference between success and failure in the efforts of any "small group of thoughtful committed citizens."

In the effort to use media to advance social change, media advocacy focuses primarily on news and paid media. Why? Because with limited resources, social change activists need to focus their attention on a small number of key policymakers and opinion leaders. With news and paid advertising, you can better target these people.

The critical element of an effective media advocacy effort is that it is strategic. This means that you always need to assess your use of media *in relation to and in support of, rather than instead of or isolated from,* other approaches. Policy struggles are not easily nor quickly won, so community organizing is an important way to build support for your desired outcome and apply pressure on those whose decisions you are trying to change. You must assess various policy options and see which have the best chance of success in your political climate, and scout out potential allies and enemies to your effort. Organizing is critical to this process.[1]

Only after you have your overall advocacy strategy in place can you begin to assess how to use media to advance that effort. This is such an important point that we call it the "prime directive" of media advocacy: You can't have a media strategy without an overall strategy. The media are just one tool to help you attain your goals, so don't let them seduce you; their power demands that you do some advance work to be sure you are using them in the most effective way.

Rule 1:
You can't have a media strategy without an overall strategy.

Working through the strategic issues outlined here will save you time and energy later in your media efforts. The perpetual questions about whether to pitch a news story, respond to breaking news, write an op-ed piece, or take on a particular interview with a journalist should always be answered in light of another question: How will doing this advance your policy objectives? If you do not have a clear answer, the potential risk of unprepared media exposure may outweigh any potential benefits.

Thinking strategically is one of the most important lessons in media advocacy—and often the most difficult thing to accomplish. This is not surprising, given that many groups have too few resources to address many complex problems. When getting through the day is sometimes a major achievement, it's no wonder that there is little time for longer-term strategic thinking about how your activities, policy objectives, and goals all fit together in a coherent vision to change the world. However, having a clear advocacy strategy in place can help make you more effective down the line by helping you focus on allocating time, money, and effort only where they will truly help advance your goals.

Here are three stories that illustrate the importance of thinking strategically before launching a media effort.

"This is an outrage."

Shortly after the passage of President Clinton's so-called welfare reform bill, a group of senior administrators in a large urban health department asked us for a presentation on media advocacy. The discussion quickly turned to the problems of welfare reform and this group's outrage about what they saw as its severe consequences. One woman said she wanted to use the media to tell people about the horrible effects that the bill would create. We said to her, "Well, what do you want people to do?" She replied that she wanted people to know the facts about the problem and how many people would be hurt. We asked, "If people knew the facts, what would you want them to do?" She said that she wanted people to get angry because of the injustice of the new policy. We asked, "If people got angry, what would you want them to do?" She replied that people had to get involved because lots of children would suffer. We asked, "If people got involved, what would you want them to do?" She finally said that she didn't know what people should do. She was angry, and her impulse was to use the media to broadcast her anger, but she did not know what needed to happen to begin to remedy the problem. Like so many of us, she was outraged but had no real alternative to put forth; in effect, she was a lonely voice disconnected from others who might have a similar concern.

"That's what they're funded to do."

A while back, we received a phone call from a national organization interested in media campaigns that might reduce teen pregnancy; they wanted to create public service campaigns to tell teens to either abstain from sex or practice safer sex. We explained that such informational approaches, known as social marketing, had not been very effective in changing important health behaviors, and that trying to sell safe sex as if you were selling a product was unlikely to produce much in the way of positive results. We argued that, rather than merely giving teens a message about pregnancy, the organization should think about training groups of youth to work through the media to advocate policy changes such as school clinics, comprehensive sex education curricula, and other local policies that might have some impact on the conditions that contribute to the problem in the first place.

The caller listened politely and then explained that the focus we suggested made sense but that the people she worked with were funded to do informational media campaigns. Then, perhaps in an unguarded moment, she said that some groups were implementing mass media campaigns with an abstinence focus even though they believed such campaigns really did not work. We asked, "Why would they use an intervention that they didn't think was effective?" She responded, "Because that's what they're funded to do." When we asked why they would do something that they know won't work just because they have the money, she replied, "That's a good question."

"We want to create awareness."

A funder called us and asked for some help in designing a mass-media effort to reduce exposure to environmental tobacco smoke. She explained that she wanted to increase awareness about the negative health effects of secondhand smoke. We suggested that, although this was a good first step, building awareness was not enough to create change; we talked to her about developing a policy focus around clean indoor air legislation, with trained community advocates working through the news media to advance these policies. We explained that an awareness-raising media campaign could amplify and propel advocates' policy work, but on its own, it wasn't likely to stimulate lasting change. She acknowledged our suggested strategy but decided that it was too controversial for her organization to change the focus to action. The funder's ultimate advertising campaign did focus on changing behavior and increasing awareness, despite the fact that their previous polling had found that levels of awareness about this issue already exceeded 80%.

Strategic Lessons

These three stories illustrate some important points about media advocacy in particular, and social change in general. First, you must know what you want to have happen in order to achieve change. If you are going to sound the alarm about welfare reform, you need to have some policy option or approach that you can put forth to address the problem. It doesn't need to be a complete solution—for example, it could be a process (e.g., convening community meetings) or a partial answer (e.g., extra support for a specific subgroup to offset the consequences of a policy change)—but it does need to be a contribution toward a more desirable situation.

Another lesson is that when programs consider the use of mass media, they often use the least powerful strategies, focused on messages to change individual behavior, rather than more powerful approaches focused on movements to advocate for policy change. In fact, funders often seem to force a focus on behaviors when a focus on policies is necessary. This puts many people in the position of implementing programs that they know to be ineffective because they fear that policy advocacy would put their jobs and funding in jeopardy. However, in fact, it is well within the legal rights of nonprofits to educate policymakers and the public about community problems and potential policy solutions.[2]

When considering what communications strategy to take, be sure to ask yourself what is the most appropriate approach: What will make the biggest difference? For instance, will it help to encourage impoverished young pregnant teens to eat more healthfully if their dietary options are limited by an abundance of fast-food outlets and a lack of grocery stores or produce stands? Perhaps advocating for a farmer's market in the neighborhood is more pragmatic than teaching teens about the importance of eating five servings of fruits and vegetables a day, when such nutritious options are not readily available. Of course, it is important to inform teens about how crucial a healthy diet is to their developing babies. But to stop there, in a neighborhood where fresh, reasonably priced produce is not available, is unfair to the very teens who are in need of help. Instead, engaging those same teens in efforts to increase the availability of fresh foods helps them demand that those in power help them have healthier babies. This blends personal responsibility with social accountability.

The third lesson is that raising awareness is not enough. You may certainly need to raise awareness of your issue to get it on the public agenda—many of the problems advocacy groups take on may not be well-known to the public or key decision makers. However, too many groups stop there. Remember that awareness is only the first step toward change, not the end result. In your planning, always go beyond awareness to action. Ask yourself, If I am successful in making people aware of this issue, what would I want them to do about it? or What is the next reasonable step that should be taken to eventually remedy this problem? Makani Themba Nixon suggests,

> Think of media advocacy as a microphone. It's an important tool. It amplifies your message and gets you heard. It can even capture your message and help make it a matter of record, but your message must support your goals and objectives. If it doesn't, it's worthless.

George Gerbner, former dean of the Annenberg School of Communication at the University of Pennsylvania, often tells the story of the Soviet dissidents in the 1970s, who concluded their underground meetings with the toast, "Here's to the success of our impossible task." Only a few years ago, one would have been crazy to predict the fall of the Berlin Wall, the defeat of pro-gun candidates in local and state elections, or an offer by tobacco companies to commit almost $400 billion to settle lawsuits from the states (and the tobacco control advocates refusing to settle). These examples show that whereas many people believe that developing strategy begins with selecting a "winnable" issue, what is winnable will change a great deal over time. Certainly, it is important to "start where the people are" by identifying issues with which community members resonate. But the key consideration in taking on an issue may not be its perceived winnability at a given time but rather the fundamental injustice of the problem and the desire to commit to a long-term strategy to address it.

In your planning, you should address five questions that form the basis for constructing an overall strategy. From this process, your specific media objectives, media messages, and media targets will flow. With your organizing partners, take the time to carefully consider and develop answers to each of these questions.

Steps for Developing Strategy

Checklist: Questions for Strategy Development

1. What is the problem?
2. What is the solution?
3. Who has the power to make the necessary change?
4. Who must be mobilized to apply pressure for change?
5. What message would convince those with the power to act for change?

	Problem Definition Makes All the Difference: *Two Approaches to the Problem of Drug Use Among Youth*	
	Approach 1	*Approach 2*
If the problem is defined as . . .	lack of information	lack of resources and alternatives
the solution becomes . . .	increase information about risks of drug use	increase social resources (e.g., mentor programs, afterschool programs)
The target for change is . . .	potential drug users	governing and corporate bodies that control resources
and the group to be mobilized is . . .	media and parents, to deliver and reinforce the information	youth and community groups, to pressure for policy change

Figure 1.1.

1. What is the problem?

Journalists, opinion leaders, policymakers, and others are always interested in this question: They want to know about the problem. Advocates are generally very knowledgeable about the problems on which they are working. Indeed, many advocates can talk at great length about problems of poverty, the environment, tobacco, guns, and so on. However, advocates are often not as adept as they should be in breaking down the problem into manageable pieces.

For example, the problem of poverty involves issues related to welfare reform, health and nutrition, employment, housing, and education. It is more effective to choose to focus on one of these issues than to talk about the larger, more intangible problem of poverty. The same problem also exists in reverse: Advocates may be so caught up in the specific details of shifting funds from one acronym-laden agency to another that they forget how to talk about the bigger problem they are trying to solve.

How you define a problem has significant impact on what solutions are considered feasible and who has domain over those solutions. For example, the problem of drug use among teenagers is often understood as a problem of lack of information; that is, if teenagers and their parents truly understood the risks of drug use, they would take action to avoid and prevent its use. This means that the solution becomes getting the right information to the right people: youth and parents. The target for change is the young person who uses or could begin using drugs, and the group to be mobilized to reach the target is parents and the media.

On the other hand, if drug use among young people is defined as a problem of lack of resources and alternatives for youth, the solution is to increase social resources that could have a positive impact on young lives (mentoring programs, afterschool recreation and enrichment programs, etc.). The means to reducing drug use among teens may not focus on drugs at all. The target for change is then the governing and corporate bodies that could allocate these resources, and the group to be mobilized includes young people themselves and the community groups that support them. (See Figure 1.1.)

ADVOCACY IN ACTION: Issue Definition

The Oakland Coalition on Alcohol Outlet Issues (CAOI) was concerned with a broad range of alcohol-related problems, including everything from littering to liver cirrhosis to violence. They were also concerned, from a social justice perspective, about the fact that poor communities of color had more liquor stores and certain types of alcohol problems than affluent white neighborhoods. However, the specific issue they settled on, which seemed most relevant for the community, was the fact that public safety decreases as the number of alcohol outlets increases. Thus, they translated the overall problem of too much alcohol and too many alcohol problems in the community into a specific issue of liquor stores constituting a threat to the safety of the community. This allowed for a clear and concise statement of the issue.

---

2. What is the solution?

Once you have developed a concise statement of your specific issue, the next question seeks to uncover the solution or approach you want to advance. After asking about the problem, journalists will always ask what you think should be done about it. A common pitfall is that people expend so much energy communicating about the problem that when the inevitable second question is asked, they are ill-prepared to answer it. Typical responses might be, "Well, it is a very complex problem with many facets, so the solution is complicated," or "The community needs to all come together," or "Parents need to take more responsibility for their children." Certainly, these responses are truthful, but they are all vague; they don't advance the issue toward a specific solution. More effective by far is to answer with a specific, implementable solution. For example, "Lead poisoning rates are increasing, and the city must spend the lead abatement funds earmarked for this problem. The public health director must put these programs on the fast track."

Your solution need not be the comprehensive set of actions that would eradicate the problem forever; it is just the next concrete step you and your group are advocating for today. Not only will this help keep you focused, but it will help get you coverage: Calling for specific actions is more interesting and newsworthy to journalists than talking about general sweeping changes.

In fact, the problems you face *are* complex, and the real solutions are long-term. But to concentrate on one small part of the solution, rather than being a cop-out, will actually advance your overall cause further in the long run.

ADVOCACY IN ACTION: A Specific Policy Solution

In Oakland, members of the Coalition on Alcohol Outlet Issues knew exactly what they wanted to have happen to reduce the problems around liquor stores. They wanted a moratorium on new liquor licenses and an ordinance to impose a fee on every liquor store in Oakland. The funds from this fee would be used for community policing programs and inspections to address the public safety problems around the liquor stores. The moratorium and tax would by no means eliminate the serious alcohol problems in the community. They would, however, begin to address the problem and provide the community with more power and resources to define their physical environment. The statement of both the problem and solution was very concise and could be presented easily in a 10- to 15-second media bite.

3. Who has the power to make the necessary change?

Once you have clearly articulated the problem and solution, assess who has the power to make the specific change that you want to see happen. In our society, people typically believe that it is primarily the person with the problem who should be responsible for changing. For example, many believe that alcohol-related problems would be prevented if only people would drink less. Similarly, childhood lead poisoning would be effectively addressed if parents did a better job of keeping children's play areas free of lead dust and keeping closer watch on their toddlers so that they do not put dusty toys in their mouths. Thus, lead poisoning is reduced to simply a problem of bad housekeeping affecting isolated families rather than a social concern affecting broad populations.

The problem with this individualistic attribution of responsibility is that in our society, the person with the problem (or "at risk" of developing it) is usually the one with the least money, the least education, the least support, and the most vulnerability to the problem. Our society's overemphasis on rugged individualism puts the burden to fix the problem on those with the fewest resources.

A fairer attribution of responsibility resides with the individual, body, group, or organization that has the decision-making power to alter policy that affects the environment in a more substantial and permanent way. Rather than educating all those at risk, the goal is to persuade a few key decision makers to change the environment in a way that reduces risk for all. For instance, if you are concerned about tobacco advertising, you could decide to institute restrictions on advertising that reaches youth, or you could continually try to educate youth about the manipulative and false claims of tobacco ads. In the former case your target is a regulatory body or corporate entity, and if you are successful, then the solution will be largely effective—ads will no longer reach youth. In the latter case, you will be required to constantly educate millions of youth, with new people entering your target group each year, and with a strategy that will not effectively influence all the people in your group, yet one that has to be continued indefinitely.

You should be as specific as you can about naming your target. In some cases, the person with the power to make the necessary change might be a single individual who holds the deciding vote on a legislative subcommittee. Even though you are only speaking to one person, the media can help you "turn up the volume" on your conversation, make the conversation public, and make you more effective.

For instance, injury prevention advocate Andrew McGuire was instrumental in promoting standards to ban flammable sleepwear for children in the early 1970s. Some 25 years later, the Consumer Product Safety Commission (CPSC) was considering relaxing that standard, which threatened to reverse the dramatic improvements in preventing childhood burns. McGuire knew that, of the three-member CPSC, one member firmly supported the old standard, one was in favor of the newer riskier standard, and the third was undecided. To put the spotlight on the issue for that one undecided commissioner, McGuire organized a news conference to demand that the CPSC maintain the previous effective standard. He gathered national fire prevention experts to speak at the conference and showed videotape of flammable pajamas burning to provide a vivid demonstration of the risks involved. The news conference was covered on network television, as well as in the *Washington Post*—the newspaper most likely to be seen by the Washington, D.C. based commissioner. When we talked to McGuire and commented on the extent of the coverage, he replied, "All that work was just to get to one person—the one member of the CPSC who we thought we could convince."

ADVOCACY IN ACTION: A Shifting Target

Your target may not remain constant throughout the policy process. For example, the Oakland Coalition on Alcohol Outlet Issues first focused on the city's Planning Commission to get their ordinance approved and then moved on to the City Council to get the ordinance implemented. As the ordinance was challenged by the alcohol industry at the state level, key state legislators then became primary targets. The lesson from Oakland, where the struggle ultimately led to the California Supreme Court, is that the target shifts and the victory is never secured until the policy has been implemented and is being effectively administered or enforced.

ADVOCACY IN ACTION: X Marks the Target

"X" was a proposed cigarette brand that many activists believed appropriated the strong, positive sentiment that young African Americans have for Malcolm X and used it to sell cigarettes. The brand was manufactured by a small Massachusetts company, Star Tobacco Corp., and marketed and distributed by Duffy Distributors. The packaging, marketing, and low price seemed lethal weapons in the tobacco industry's efforts to hook more young African Americans.

The effort to stop X brand cigarettes evolved out of a network of activists who had been mobilizing communities of color around the targeted marketing of tobacco and alcohol products. Brenda Bell-Caffee, director of the California African American Tobacco Education Network, saw a message about X on a computer mailing list for tobacco control advocates and immediately alerted her colleagues. In the group's assessment, the two small companies that made and marketed the product were more reachable, winnable targets than any relevant public agencies. The strategy was, therefore, crafted to mobilize pressure and shame these companies into revoking the brand.

The group worked to shame the target by emphasizing two messages: X brand (whether purposely or not) defamed an important leader and cultural icon, Malcolm X; and it was packaged in a way that was sure to attract African American youths. The group gave the companies 10 days to withdraw the brand.

Media played a critical role in pressuring the companies to respond. Activists got the word out to both African American and corporate-owned media outlets, and articles on X appeared in more than 100 newspapers nationwide. Succumbing to national pressure, Duffy Distributors issued a statement one day after the deadline, which—without any admission of wrongdoing—detailed their commitment to withdraw the brand. X brand cigarettes were pulled from distribution.

Checklist: Key Questions in Choosing a Target

1. Who or what institution has power to solve the problem and grant your demands? Identify which is the most important target for achieving your policy goal.
2. Who must you get to first before those above?
3. What are the strengths and weaknesses of each potential target?
4. Which targets are appointed? Elected? Private?
5. How do you have power or influence with them? (As voters, consumers, stockholders, taxpayers, shaming, etc.)
6. What is their self-interest?
7. Who would have jurisdiction if you redefined the issue (e.g., turned a tobacco advertising issue into a fair business practices issue)? Does this help you?

4. Who must be mobilized to apply pressure for change?

Change is difficult to achieve because those who are the targets typically benefit from the status quo or are under great pressure from those who do. Although those with the power to make the required change are obviously the primary target, you must also focus on a critical secondary target: those who can apply the pressure to make sure that change is made. Effective coalitions chart the self-interest of each potential ally and target, assessing their depth of concern and risk in supporting the initiative, to shape an effective message to draw them in—or neutralize them.

Creating change often requires long-term, consistent pressure on the person, body, group, or organization that needs to make the change. Community groups and other interested parties must be mobilized to apply pressure. For example, ACT-UP, an AIDS activist group advocates moving new drugs through the FDA approval process more quickly to get them into the hands of people with AIDS and HIV. They routinely mobilize committed advocates to apply pressure to FDA officials, pharmaceutical companies, and a range of governmental agencies to make the changes they deem necessary to address the AIDS epidemic.

In developing strategy, consider that there are a number of roles for different groups and individuals to play. Not everyone is in front of the camera or writing op-ed pieces. In addition to community organizations and community activists, there are also researchers, educators, social and health service agency professionals, and business people. Because so many of the issues relating to social change are controversial, some groups, for one reason or another, cannot be publicly involved. However, these groups can provide important background functions that could be key to the success of your initiatives. For example, health and social welfare departments can supply data, provide advance notice of reports that will be released, and provide resources for community forums or training sessions. Researchers can provide help with analyzing and interpreting data and might serve as experts on specific issues. In sum, identify a wide range of roles that can fit with the abilities of the various groups you want to mobilize to advance your issue.

ADVOCACY IN ACTION: Mobilizing the Community

In Oakland, it took four years and some compromise to implement the alcohol outlet ordinance, which assesses a $600 annual fee on liquor stores. To sustain this kind of effort, it was necessary to have committed advocates keep applying pressure on the decision makers to do the right thing. At every key point—city council meetings or legislative sessions—the organizers of the ordinance effort were successful in turning people out. This made the event more newsworthy and showed the decision makers that people cared about the issue and were going to hold them accountable. At the final city council vote, the pro-ordinance forces filled the hearing room with people who had signs indicating the neighborhoods or organizations they were representing. The city council members saw people from their own district who were there to watch how they voted. This is a personal and very important kind of pressure. Also, the community interest made the issue more newsworthy and increased media coverage, creating even more pressure.

5. What message would convince those with the power to act for change?

Now that you know who the focus of your advocacy effort is and what you want them to do, you can begin to develop the message that will help convince your target to make the change you want.

There are varying degrees of message development. Well-funded issue campaigns or political candidates might develop messages for voters through sophisticated concept development, focus group research, and public opinion polling. They might test out the effects of specific words, finding, for example, that people are more likely to support controls on *hand*guns than on *guns*.[3] Or they might shape their message, as the Republican Party did, based on research that showed that "individual programs have friends. Bureaucracies and bureaucrats don't. Therefore, focus the general rhetorical attack on the 'Washington bureaucracy.' "[4]

Deciding on your message is a developmental process. Sure, you know that you want to prevent violence, provide access to quality child care, or preserve old growth forests, but these are goals from which messages evolve. The message is really a way to articulate your goal to a variety of audiences in a meaningful and compelling way.

Keep in mind a few points. First, different messages must be developed to appeal to different audiences. For example, your message for the other advocacy groups you are trying to mobilize will be different from a message designed to get the attention of a specific policymaker or legislative body.

Second, messages can change over time. In the initial stages, your message might have to focus more on increasing awareness of the problem. However, as time goes on, you will want to refocus on the solutions or policy alternatives you are putting forth. Your message needs to be dynamic because the political environment of your problem and solution will be in constant flux. Unless you can adapt your message accordingly, you will not be fully effective.

Third, consider who your spokespeople will be, because, as the old saying goes, the messenger is the message. Credibility and legitimacy of those giving the message is critical, and you may need a different spokesperson for the different groups at whom you aim the message. In Houston, advocates we spoke with who had worked to preserve affirmative action in the city's contracting processes noted that the popular white mayor was an ideal spokesperson for media appearances aimed at businesspeople and voters overall, whereas leaders from the African American and Latino communities were good spokespeople for mobilizing members of their own communities.

The Role of Public Opinion

The first step in the message development process is to better understand how people are thinking about and talking about the issue. Too often, advocates assume others understand the issue the same way that they do; or they believe that if they could just make people aware of the facts, then these people would become supporters. But in fact, whereas your issue may be very high on your own agenda, it may not even be on the radar screen of those you seek to influence. Even if they are aware of it, you cannot assume that even your potential supporters are thinking about the issue in the way that is most consistent with your goals.

Perhaps, a useful test of your assumptions about how people perceive your issue might be to put it to the Uncle Charley/Sister Susan test. What happens when you ask an uninitiated family member what he or she thinks about your issue? The results might surprise you. For example, we were taken aback when a family member of one of the authors took the side of the tobacco industry regarding the appropriateness of payments to compensate smokers for tobacco-related diseases. "After all," he said, "there's a warning label on every package." He didn't think about the billions of dollars the companies have spent to make their products seem fun and harmless, effectively overwhelming the small, technical, black-and-white warning labels. The bottom line is, you cannot assume that people understand and think about the issue in the same way you do.

Pollster Ethel Klein has a wonderful metaphor she uses in discussing public opinion, calling it a "public conversation." Klein explains that advocacy groups try to move the public conversation from point A to point B. However, they make a common error in only focusing on point B—where they want to end up—and largely ignoring point A—how people are currently thinking and talking about the issue. The problem becomes evident when, in retrospect, it becomes clear that point B is much too far from the current discussion to realistically expect such a shift. For example, it would be difficult to move public opinion to support a ban on handguns (point B) if people did not already agree that these guns were a hazard (point A).

How does public opinion research—understanding where the general conversation is on your issue—relate to the overall goal of reaching a specific target? The three targets are a hierarchy, with each level influenced by the others. The primary target is influenced by the special group that it answers to: Politicians are influenced by voters in their districts, company boards of directors are influenced by their stockholders, school boards are influenced by parents, and so on. Both the primary and secondary targets might be influenced by public opinion, but, even though we are talking about mass media here, rarely is the general public a main target for media advocates. This is because advocates usually direct the message to the primary target, using the mass media so the target can be held accountable to the whole community. Making the demand and response part of the public record, via the news, is what puts pressure on the target.

There are occasions when media advocates are interested in moving general public opinion, but even then, it is usually some narrowed portion of the public. For example, on statewide policy efforts, it may be important to know how voters are talking about an issue so that the primary target can be approached in terms that resonate with supporters. Public opinion research can be enormously useful in these circumstances—not to determine what your goal is (presumably, you already know that) but to help you figure out how to talk about it in terms that resonate for the public. You can use public opinion research to learn the most promising way to get from where the public is on an issue to the specific policy you want them to support.

Find out where the public conversation is before deciding where you can realistically expect it to end up.

It is important, then, to find out where the public conversation is before deciding where you can realistically expect it to end up. Assessing public opinion involves conducting focus groups and polls. Increasingly, advocacy groups are becoming more sophisticated in using these tools that have been so vital to political campaigns. Also, in recent years, philanthropic foundations are gaining an increasing appreciation of the importance of gathering this type of intelligence to shape strategy. Here is one illustration of how this process of intelligence gathering works.

For example, the California Wellness Foundation (TCWF) is investing in a 10-year initiative to reduce the level of violence among youth in California. One of its key goals is to reduce the availability of handguns to youth, and TCWF has developed several policies to support this goal. In focus groups around the state, it was discovered that people were not aware that guns were the leading cause of death among youth in California. Furthermore, when people learned this, their responsiveness to various gun policies increased.

The information from the focus groups was tested in a statewide survey of registered voters. The poll validated the key point: When people learned that guns were the No. 1 killer of youth in the state, their support for gun control policies significantly increased. It was also evident from the poll that people differentiated among guns in general, handguns, and long guns and that policies to limit handguns enjoyed higher support than more general gun control policies. In addition, the poll was very helpful in identifying sub-groups who were strong supporters of handgun control and might be mobilized to take supportive actions.

As a result of focus groups and polling, several key decisions were made in designing a public education campaign on the gun issue:

- Time for the paid public education campaign was purchased to reach women ages 18 to 45, who had been found to be the strongest supporters of handgun control policies. The idea was to motivate existing supporters to take specific action that would increase their level of commitment and support the overall goals of the campaign.
- Based on testing, the message of the campaign emphasized two key points: Handguns are the leading cause of death among youth in the state, and there are far too many of these guns.
- Testing of voter perceptions showed that people needed to be made aware that youth suffer from the problem of gun violence and are not just perpetrators of the problem.

Some important points require mentioning here. First, only registered voters were included in the focus groups and polls. This often raises questions among community groups and grassroots activists about neglecting the voices of those who might not be registered to vote. In this case, politicians and other policymakers were the target, and they are influenced by what voters think. Polls and focus groups that report their findings based on registered voters have much greater impact on these targets than more inclusive polls.

Second, the campaign planners invested in research to explore different ways that voters were thinking about the issue. This is a two-step process. The focus group setting allows for more qualitative and deeper discussion of the issues. Comments can be probed to better understand the emotional loading behind the response and body language can also be observed. But because focus groups are very small (usually no more than 12 people), it is difficult to reliably generalize to larger populations. Therefore, it is important to test out the focus group findings in a larger scientifically drawn sample that explores whether the findings of the focus groups are accurate for the larger population.

Third, the campaign did not seek to reach opponents and convert them to a new position. Rather, it sought to reinforce and mobilize those already supportive to take a specific action. It was hoped that those without firm views could be swayed to the cause, and this is certainly an important secondary audience. On emotional issues, it simply is not possible to convert large numbers of people to a different ideological position than the one they have. Regardless of the level of resources a group has, there will never be enough to convert true believers to the opposite position. To ignore this fact would be costly and strategically unwise.

Elements of an
Effective Message

The most important thing about developing your message is to keep it simple. A good message uses concise, direct language to convey at least three elements. First, there is the clear statement of concern: for example, the fact that there are too many liquor stores in the community. The second part of the message represents the value dimension, such as the threat to community cohesion and family well-being that the concentration of liquor stores fosters.

The third part elucidates the policy objective, say, a moratorium on new liquor stores within a certain district. It is as important to be able to describe the policy solution as it is to describe the problem. Advocates tend to spend too much of their time talking about the problem and trying to raise awareness and not enough of their time stating what needs to be done and who should do it. Change is about channeling awareness into action and that means mobilizing people around a solution.

ADVOCACY IN ACTION: When Media Attention Isn't Necessary

A group of young people in San Francisco's Bayview-Hunter's Point neighborhood conducted a survey of young people's needs regarding the recreational facilities and programs available to them. The survey showed that many facilities were unclean and unsafe and also lacked some programs the youth wanted, such as mentoring and tutoring programs, at their recreation facilities. The youth group decided to ask the San Francisco Board of Supervisors to free up money to make the necessary changes. The Supervisors agreed to meet with the group, listened to their requests, and agreed to visit the facilities to see the conditions firsthand. In this case, drawing media attention to the issue was not necessary to achieving the group's goals. However, the young people continued to watch to be sure the Supervisors followed through, and they developed a flexible media plan to either praise or censure the Board, depending on whether Supervisors honored their commitments.

Summary

Our first rule is: You can't have a media strategy without an overall strategy. To develop strategy, focus on an issue that you are concerned about, choose specific policies to address that issue, and know who has the power to implement these policies. Because creating change is a long-term process with much resistance, it is critical to identify and develop relationships with committed activists and supporters who can be mobilized to apply pressure over the long run. Then, you can begin to focus on the key messages that will underlie all your advocacy efforts.

Not until you have done all this advance work should you even consider whether a mass media effort is appropriate to support your goals. Laying the strategic groundwork will dictate the rest of your approach. For instance, if the policy target agrees to meet with your group, listens, and responds as you had hoped, you don't need to attract news attention to bring pressure to bear on that target. Instead, you might consider writing an op-ed piece to congratulate the policymaker for doing the right thing for your community. In another case, the strategic planning process might reveal that one specific corporate executive is your key target, and you discover that she reads the *Chicago Tribune*, not the *Sun-Times*. This gives you important information for focusing your media work on the media outlet most likely to reach your target; you can conserve resources and increase efficiency.

Notes

1. Resources on organizing and community development are listed in Appendix B.

2. Resources on nonprofit lobbying are listed in Appendix B.

3. Wallack, L. (in press). "Strategies for reducing youth violence: Media, community, and policy," in Jamner, M., & Stokols, D. (eds.), *Promoting human wellness: New frontiers for research, practice, and policy.* Berkeley, CA: University of California Press.

4. *Communication strategy for the upcoming budget battle,* a memo by F. Luntz, is excerpted in Toner, R. (1995, February 5). Attention! All sales reps for the Contract with America!, *New York Times,* Sec. 4, p. 7.

2

GETTING TO KNOW THE MEDIA

---◆---

The newspapers! Sir, they are the most villainous, licentious, abominable, infernal—Not that I ever read them! No, I make it a rule never to look into a newspaper.

Richard Brinsley Sheridan, The Critic, *1779*

---◆---

We are often surprised by advocates who say they want to put the power of the media to work for their issues, yet go on to admit to us, "I never watch TV news—it's so superficial." Likewise, how many advocates read *The New York Times* but never pick up their own local newspaper? Although we understand the frustrations that lead to avoiding the news, such attitudes are counterproductive when you try to work with local journalists on your issues.

If you want to be taken seriously as a credible source for reporters, you need to take the media seriously. This means the media in all their forms—even if you think your local broadcasts are sensationalistic tabloid shows and your local paper is a biased rag. No matter what you think of these news sources, they are influencing the way people see their world, understand your issue, and evaluate the solutions they are willing to support. You can't afford to keep your head in the sand about such powerful sources of influence.

> **Rule 2:**
> *If you want to be taken seriously as a credible source*
> *for reporters, you need to take the media seriously.*

You need to know what's in the news, why it's there, and how it's being discussed. Even if you regularly read your local paper and watch the local news, you may be able to make these activities more productive by bearing your advocacy goals in mind as you do.

Fortunately, getting to know the media is not hard. It merely takes being more conscious about reading and watching the news and following up by making contact with journalists. This boils down to three steps: **monitor the media**, **create a media list**, and **develop relationships with journalists**.

Monitor the Media   As an activist, your first step—and your ongoing commitment—should be to monitor the media. This simply means reading the paper, watching the news, and/or listening to radio news with a critical perspective.

Decide which media sources to monitor.

Remember, your prime objective is to reach the target of your advocacy efforts—the person or organization with the power to make the change you seek. This means you should pay attention to the media sources that your target is likely to pay attention to. The objective of media monitoring is to discover whether and how your issue is being reported in the news sources to which your target is most likely to respond.

Of course, you have secondary audiences too—those who can be mobilized to bring pressure to bear on your target. These may be parents, voters, health professionals, workers, youth, or other groups. The general public is also an important secondary target. So other media sources may be appropriate for those audiences, and it pays to be aware of how the issue is being reported in those sources. You will benefit by monitoring as many sources as you can.

Develop a critical eye as a news consumer.

Once you have chosen the news outlets you will monitor, begin to read, watch, and listen to them. Although you don't need to be as rigorous as if you were doing a scientific analysis of media content, you do want to be alert to the coverage on your issue. You have more substantial objectives than merely being informed about what's news each day; you will have several questions in mind. Here are a few to consider as you go through the news:

1. **Is your issue being covered?** Sometimes the first hurdle is getting your issue into the news at all. Often advocates are frustrated that the news covers dramatic stories that don't affect many local people, such as the birth of septuplets, while neglecting issues that may have an impact on more people, such as prevention of asthma among young children. You need to know whether or not your issue is in the news.

2. **If your issue is not being covered, are other issues being covered that relate to your issue?** It is often possible to piggyback on a related topic to

attract attention to your issue. For example, if your issue is sexually transmitted diseases (a topic receiving little coverage), note how related issues, such as teen pregnancy, AIDS, or sex education, are being covered.

3. What are the main themes and arguments presented on various sides of the issue? If your issue is covered, it's important to consider *how* it's covered. This will give you a comprehensive view of how the topic has been treated in the past so that you can better anticipate how it will be covered in the future and how to help shape or "frame" that coverage. (For more on framing, see Chapter 4.)

4. Who is reporting on your issue or stories related to it? Be sure to note the names of journalists who are reporting comprehensively on the subject, as well as those who need more information to improve their reporting. This will help build your media lists.

5. Who appear as spokespeople on your issue? Pay attention not just to names, but to types: Are teachers or students speaking out on an education issue, or only administration officials? Are politicians being quoted to the exclusion of parents on issues related to family welfare? What organizations are represented in the news coverage? Who are the spokespeople for the opposition, and what does their presence convey about the other side of this issue? Knowing who is speaking on the issue can help you identify gaps to be filled and anticipate arguments you'll need to counter.

6. Who is writing op-ed pieces or letters to the editor on your issue? Which side are they taking? Opinion pieces have particular impact because these sections are considered to reveal the "pulse" of the community. Policy-makers often turn to opinion sections to see what the community is concerned about and what positions people are taking. (See Chapter 7 for editorial page strategies.)

7. Are any solutions to the problem presented? Often news does a good job of describing problems but may not include solutions. Or, the solutions included may not be those you agree with. You need to know this so you can plan how best to inform journalists about what you think should be done about your issue.

8. Who is named or implied as having responsibility for solving the problem? Is our target named in the coverage? You will need to know whether the news spotlight is already fixed on your target or whether getting that attention will be one of your challenges.

9. What stories, facts, or perspectives could help improve the case for your side? While advocates tend to put a lot of faith in facts, facts must be combined with compelling personal stories to move people to action. Whose

---

Checklist: Monitoring the Media

1. Is your issue being covered?
2. If not, are other issues being covered that relate to your issue?
3. What are the main themes and arguments presented on various sides of the issue?
4. Who is reporting on your issue or stories related to it?
5. Who are appearing as spokespeople on your issue?
6. Who is writing op-ed pieces or letters to the editor on your issue? Which side are they taking?
7. Are any solutions presented to the problem?
8. Who is named or implied as having responsibility for solving the problem? Is your target named in the coverage?
9. What stories, facts, or perspectives could help improve the case for your side?
10. What's missing from the news coverage of your issue?

---

stories and perspectives could be included in the coverage to help motivate decision makers?

10. What's missing from the news coverage of your issue? People are so used to taking the news at face value that they seldom think about what is *not* included in news coverage. An important part of monitoring the media is applying your intimate knowledge of the issue to determine what is not there that should be. For instance, in coverage of child safety, most articles focus on what parents can do to keep their children safe; there is relatively little coverage of policy issues, such as mandatory fencing around pools or uniform attachments for car seats, that would help prevent injuries among a larger number of children. Recognizing what is missing from the news is extremely important, and it takes some practice. After all, it is easier to see what is there than what is *not* there. Knowing what's missing will help you fill these gaps in your future media work.

Create a Media List   As you monitor the media, begin to create a media list or expand any existing lists. Your personalized media list will give you a starting point for all contacts with journalists, whether you are faxing a news release to every reporter in the area who might be interested or trying to choose the one best reporter to whom you'll pitch a special story.

Your list should include names, affiliations, addresses, e-mail addresses, and phone and fax numbers for all local (and some regional or national) journalists covering your issue. It can be an electronic database or as simple as a series of Rolodex cards. Compiling and updating such a list requires considerable attention, but you can't operate without it. Bear in mind that a list can go out of date quickly: addresses change, reporters and editors move to different outlets, publications and stations alter their formats and sometimes go out of business. Keeping a list up-to-date can be a big job; some organizations may want to share the task with other organizations working on similar issues. (See *Try It Out* at the end of this chapter.)

Start with the names you cull from monitoring.

As you monitor the media, you should note which reporters cover your issue or stories related to it; in particular, highlight those who do a good job on the subject. These notes will form the core of your media list.

Expand your list with other sources.

Consult local media directories to gather more names. Check the masthead of local papers for names of editors and other staff and phone numbers of specific departments. Check the news outlet's website or call local stations and publications and ask who would be most interested in stories on your issue. Include regional outlets and wire services. TV and radio public affairs departments often create listings of local media numbers that they distribute to community members who request them. The problem with these lists is that they often concentrate on public affairs directors rather than news departments, but they can be a good start.

You can also purchase commercial media lists; they are designed for public relations firms and usually cost around $300 per year but can be helpful as a starting point if you think the investment will pay off. We provide a few suggested resources in the Appendix. If you can't afford a media resource book yourself, ask a larger organization if you can have their old one. Such resources are typically updated quarterly, so an old one isn't necessarily too out-of-date.

Keep track of personal contacts.

Build your media list by updating it regularly from the records you keep of all media contacts—every telephone call, meeting, conference, or interview. Any time a reporter calls you, or vice versa, be sure to make a note of it in your media list. Note the subject of the story, what information you provided, whom else you referred the reporter to, any other important points, and any follow-up needed. A sample Media Contact Form, which you can use or adapt for your own media list, is shown in Figure 2.1.

Sample Media Contact Form

Date _____   Contact initiated by: _____

Time _____   Staff _____   Media _____

Follow-Up Needed: _____

Follow-Up Needed By: _____

Follow-Up Completed: _____

_____

Name   _____

Title   _____

Affiliation   _____

Address   _____

                  _____

Phone   _____

Fax   _____

                  TV ❏   Print ❏   Radio ❏   Online ❏

Request/Comments/Notes: _____

_____

_____

_____

_____

_____

_____

❏ Add to Media List   ❏ Added to Media List: Date _____

Figure 2.1

Develop Relationships With Journalists

Your list will be even more effective if you cultivate relationships with journalists. If you feel intimidated by this, as many people do, remember that reporters are just professionals doing their job. Their task is to be skeptical and objective so they can get all sides of an issue, and they need your perspective to make their stories complete. If you get to know what their interests and needs are, you will get better coverage of your issue, and the reporters will get a credible, reliable source, which they value.

How do you start building relationships with journalists? If you're just setting up a media list, send an introductory letter to every reporter you add to the list. Let them know the issues for which you can serve as a resource. Enclose fact sheets and your business card or a preprinted Rolodex card for their files. You can even invite the reporter to lunch or to tour the agency or neighborhood where you work.

As you continue your media monitoring, you will see stories that are particularly well done. Use this as an opportunity to establish or expand your relationship with that journalist. Write to the reporter or producer to let him or her know that your group is concerned about the issue covered. Commend the reporter/producer for being responsive to such an important issue. Use the letter as an opportunity to introduce your organization and its mission, and send an information packet along.

Bear in mind that it is better to compliment the journalist by saying his or her story was balanced, thorough, interesting, or fair than by saying it was a "good" or "helpful" story. You cannot go wrong if you praise the reporter for following journalistic values of objectivity and balance, whereas you might raise hackles if you thank him or her for doing your organization a favor with a "good" story. Remember, it is not the journalist's job to help you out; it's his or her job to report the news.

Although journalists get a lot of exposure, they generally don't get a lot of feedback. One TV anchor told a group of nonprofit representatives that although he did about two positive stories a week, amounting to over 100 stories a year, he never got a call from a viewer about any of the positive stories—just criticisms about the negative stories. A *Los Angeles Times* reporter said, "The things we write may be very influential, but it feels like it's put out in a bottle in the ocean for the amount of feedback we get. Two or three responses feels like an avalanche."[1]

Chances are good that if you write a simple letter about a well-done story, or leave a message on a reporter's voice mail, he or she will remember you when you call back with a story idea. Positive reinforcement is a good way to establish rapport.

Of course, you can also respond to specific reporters when you *don't* like the way they've covered an issue. Just bear in mind your overall goal: getting to know reporters so you can help them do a better job covering your issue. You want to build long-term relationships and become viewed as a credible and useful resource. Be sure to offer any criticisms or suggestions accordingly. For instance, you could send a note that suggests a new angle for a future story, rather than attacking a story that is already yesterday's news. Attaching a fact sheet or information packet is a good way to prove your willingness to help the reporter, not just criticize.

Ultimately, your objective is to be a known and trusted resource to journalists. This means providing them with material they can rely on and connecting them to interesting people with good stories to tell. When reporters are in a time crunch and can only make a couple of calls to fill the gaps in their story, you want to be the one they call.

Ultimately, your objective is to be a known and trusted resource to journalists.

ADVOCACY IN ACTION: Develop Relationships With Reporters

In July 1995, the Regents of the University of California voted to eliminate the consideration of gender, race, or ethnicity in admissions, hiring, and contracting in the nine-campus system. The process leading up to the decision was hotly contested and became a focus of national attention. The controversy was fueled by the opposition of the university faculty, as well as by students and the administration.

When some faculty at the university organized to challenge the Regents' decision to eliminate affirmative action, they developed a media strategy to complement their organizing efforts. The first thing they did was find out who was writing about the controversy and how they were presenting the issue. In some cases, they found the story being covered by higher education reporters as part of their usual beat. In other cases, the issue was being covered by political reporters because it involved the governor and his presidential ambitions. A few papers used a general assignment reporter.

Ultimately, the faculty worked most closely with the education reporters because it was these reporters who were more knowledgeable about the complex issues being advanced by the faculty. The political reporters, on the other hand, were concerned primarily with the political scorecard of who was winning and who was losing. The faculty decided not to use valuable time trying to persuade the political reporters to cover the story or trying to reframe the way it was covered. The result was that the faculty group focused on the education reporters and ultimately provided them with information that led to several front page stories in two major papers.

It's About Time: Typical Deadlines for News Outlets

It helps to know the kinds of deadlines daily reporters work under. For local TV, the deadline to have the story finished is about two hours before the broadcast. This means a 3 p.m. deadline for a 5 p.m. show, 9 p.m. for an 11 p.m. newscast. The best time to call a TV assignment desk is between 6 and 8:30 in the morning, before the 9 or 10 a.m. story meeting in most newsrooms. The worst time to call to pitch a story is after 3 p.m., when the whole newsroom is in a rush to finalize that day's newscasts.

Print deadlines vary, depending on the frequency of publication. Many daily newspapers in major cities are printed in multiple editions aimed at different parts of the metropolitan area; they may also have late and early editions, and each of these versions of the paper has a different deadline. Furthermore, deadlines may change daily as news breaks. A reporter at a morning paper may have a general guideline of 6 p.m. for routine stories but may have until 8 or even 10 p.m. to file a late-breaking story. Feel free to ask reporters what their deadline is when they call you; they will appreciate anything you can do to help them get the material they need in time for them to do the story.

In general, late morning or early afternoon tends to be the best time to call reporters at most daily newspapers, as they are still collecting information for the day's stories and not yet facing the late-afternoon rush to meet their deadline. But respect the time crunch when you call a reporter; always ask whether he or she is on deadline, and if the answer is yes, offer to call back at a better time.

Checklist: Who's Who in Newsrooms

When getting to know the people who make up the news media, you need to know who does what in the newsroom. Here are some typical people you'll find at most news outlets.

Assignment Editor or City Desk Editor:	Coordinates the day-to-day assignment of stories. Random calls to the newsroom are directed to this desk. If you can get to know an assignment or city desk editor's likes and dislikes, you'll have made a strong and useful contact at your local media outlet.
Editor:	Coordinates and assigns stories for his or her section of a newspaper or magazine. City editors handle news assignments for the urban area; publications may also have editors responsible for entertainment, arts, sports, business, the environment, and so on.
Managing Editor:	In charge of editors and operations of the whole newspaper.
Producer:	In network television, a **story producer** researches, writes, interviews, and oversees the camera crew and editing process for stories. He or she works closely with reporters and, in some cases, does much of the work to create a story. However, in local news, most reporters do this for themselves. The **show producer** decides which stories will appear on the news and in what order and works closely with the writers who create the anchor's scripts. The **executive producer** is roughly equivalent to the managing editor at a newspaper.
Reporters:	In the print media, reporters are writers. On TV and radio, they're the voices you hear reporting the news and generally the main gatherers of that news. Cultivate relationships with reporters, both staff and freelance, who know your organization, who understand its purpose, and who have the respect of editors and producers.
Public Affairs Director:	The contact at radio and TV stations responsible for airing public service announcements and free-speech messages and general community relations (arranging a tour of the newsroom, for instance).
Calendar Editor:	Responsible for events listings, announcements, and, with few exceptions, a vital source of free publicity. If your event is for community members, send a one-page media advisory specifying the basics to the calendar editor.
Freelance Writers, Photographers (stringers), and Producers:	Freelancers generally write or produce news for a variety of news outlets without being employed by any single outlet. Many editors and producers have a regular group of freelancers with whom they work frequently. Establish relationships with freelancers in the same way you do with staff writers and reporters.

A Word About PR Firms

Some groups with adequate resources might consider using a public relations firm to track coverage of their issue, develop media lists, and periodically release a report or publicize some event. Although a good PR agency can be a very useful resource to supplement your media work, we feel strongly that it is critical for advocates to be directly and personally involved in media efforts.

Only you can build effective relationships with reporters. Journalists respond differently to PR agents (whom they disparagingly call "flacks") than to "real people" with real expertise and experience on an issue. Although a PR professional may be able to help point you to reporters covering your topic, you must take the time to become a prized source to those reporters.

Our experience is that PR firms are excellent at logistics: helping to set up news conferences, placing op-ed pieces, getting reporters to turn out for events, and similar kinds of activities. They can provide you a view of the "media territory" and a quick understanding about how the news-making process works. Some firms may provide on-camera training and contribute insights into message development.

PR firms, however, are not experts on your issue and may have different ideas about what constitutes success than you do. The firm wants to get your story covered (and collect the clips) but will likely be less concerned about whether the policy issue gets covered the way you framed it. They tend to assume that getting your name (or organization's name) in the paper is an appropriate measure of success. Also, PR firms may not have the same political orientation and long-range policy goals you do, which can cause you to lose sight of the strategic purpose of your media work.

Unless you find a unique group of PR professionals to work with (and there are some), we suggest that you resist the temptation to relinquish any control over substance to PR firms. The effort and time you spend developing relationships, shaping strategy, and talking with reporters about your issue will more than repay itself in much richer coverage than would otherwise be possible.

Summary

Our second rule is: **If you want to be taken seriously as a credible source for reporters, you need to take the media seriously.** This means that you must become an astute observer of the news media. Monitor your local media to better understand whether your issues or related ones are being covered, how they are being covered, who is covering them, and how these issues can be framed to be more supportive of your policy objectives. The monitoring activity is a good way to start your media list and identify journalists you'll want to contact in the future.

To build productive relationships with reporters, you must understand the realities and limitations of the news business. In the next chapter, we introduce the basics of what news is and how to get media attention to your stories.

Note _____

1. Myron Levin's presentation to The American Society of Addiction Medicine, Marina del Rey, California, November 7, 1998.

TRY IT OUT: INSTANT MEDIA LIST

This activity takes about 30 minutes to do and is a good group activity for youth and adults to work on together. In half an hour, you'll have the beginnings of your own media list.

Step 1: Collect newspapers.

Get one copy of each newspaper where you'd like to see stories about your issue appear. Include the papers that you think the decision makers in your area pay attention to and the papers that community members you want to mobilize read. (If you only have one newspaper in your area, get several copies of it.)

Step 2: Make an information sheet for each paper.

Use a blank sheet of paper for each newspaper. At the top, list the newspaper's name, its address, its central phone and fax numbers, and two key names, such as city desk editor and opinion page or letters editor. You can get this information from the masthead, usually found on the second or third page of the paper or on the editorial page. (You can simply tape the masthead to the top of your page.) Leave space below this information for reporters' names, headlines, and notes. (See Sample Information Sheet for Instant Media List Exercise, Figure 2.2.)

Step 3: Cull reporters' names.

Look through each paper for articles that relate to your topic or to issues similar to your topic. For each article, write down the byline (name of the person who wrote the article) on the information sheet you created in Step 2. (Leave a space to add the direct phone line for each reporter by calling the newspaper for these numbers later.) The idea is to identify reporters who might be interested in your topic, based on other stories they've written. For instance, crime reporters might be interested in stories about gun control or violence prevention programs.

(continued)

Be creative. If you see a connection to your topic in a story, even if it is not obvious, include the reporter on the list, and make a note of the connection. <u>Later, you can send a note to the reporter explaining your connection, so the reporter will be aware the next time a story like yours comes up</u>. For instance, one group we worked with on child care issues noticed that the impact on children was not mentioned in front-page coverage of flood stories one wet winter. They made a note to contact reporters working on the human- interest angle of natural disaster stories and ask them to cover the impact of the disaster on education and child care.

Step 4: Keep building the list over time.

When you read any paper in the days to come, add names to the media list. These are the people to whom you will send news releases and pitch stories.

The San Francisco Chronicle
901 Mission St.
San Francisco, CA 94103-2988

415-777-1111 Main switchboard   415-777-7018 Editorial pages phone
415-777-7100 City news desk   415-543-7708 Editorial pages fax
415-896-1107 Newsroom fax   chronletters@sfgate.com

Reporter name: _____   Story date: _____

Headline/topic: _____

Notes: _____

Reporter name: _____   Story date: _____

Headline/topic: _____

Notes: _____

Reporter name: _____   Story date: _____

Headline/topic: _____

Notes: _____

Reporter name: _____   Story date: _____

Headline/topic: _____

Notes: _____

Figure 2.2. Sample Information Sheet for Instant Media List Exercise

3

THINKING LIKE A JOURNALIST
Getting Attention

—————————◆•—————————

To gain the media's attention, you can't just say something; you have to DO something.

Russel Sciandra, tobacco control advocate

—————————◆•—————————

To be effective in working through the news media, you must be pragmatic about how the news works and what you need to do to be part of it. You need to learn to think like a journalist, to look for good stories, and to be able to bring them to journalists' attention.

Frustrated advocates often complain about lack of coverage for their issue or specific news event. They consider their work to be extremely important; they don't understand why journalists ignore it or provide only cursory coverage.

If they checked with some journalists, they would quickly realize three key points about the reality of what news is. First, news is a competition, and the challenge of that competition changes every day. Back in 1922, journalist Walter Lippmann observed, "All the reporters in the world working all the hours of the day could not witness all the happenings in the world."[1] There is more news than there are resources to cover that news, so the degree to which your story is newsworthy will depend on other stories of interest that day.

ADVOCACY IN ACTION: Up Against Unbeatable Competition

A group in Los Angeles was advocating for changes in alcohol control policies. They planned a news conference to highlight their concerns; they sent out news releases, followed up with phone calls; they arranged to have some good visuals and materials to provide at the news conference. Despite all the work they did, they did not get the attention or visibility they wanted. What did they do wrong? Well, how could they possibly have known that on the day of their news conference, the verdict in the O. J. Simpson criminal trial would be announced? On some other day, this group might have been the lead story on the 6 o'clock news and a banner story in the metro section of the next day's newspaper. On the day of the Simpson verdict, however, they were up against unbeatable competition.

A second important reality checkpoint is that the definition of news is somewhat arbitrary. This is not to say that there are not some very well-defined basic conventions about what makes something newsworthy. Such conventions exist, and we review them below. However, there is no clear, succinct answer to the question of what is news. In fact, it is not uncommon for an assignment editor or news director to assert, "News is whatever I say it is." Although this may seem arrogant, it is simply an explicit acknowledgment of the arbitrary nature of news. The lesson is that news is partly shaped by the personal interests of those who report the news.

A third reality checkpoint is that news is a business. Most news organizations are careful to keep direct moneymaking concerns away from the newsroom—advertising departments are carefully isolated from the news selection process, and most journalists would proudly say they would not hesitate to expose nefarious corporate practices, even if the target of the exposé was a major advertiser. However, the business limitations of news are far more subtle than such explicit influence. When news is a business, it means that entertainment and human interest values become more important than public service or education values. News becomes shaped by the same pressures that trivialize debate in the political arena. News becomes what people want to hear about rather than what they should hear about.

For advocates who complain that their important story on homelessness did not get covered, whereas a story about ankle sprains suffered by those who use expensive running shoes did, these realities of news selection can be frustrating. However, this should be seen as a challenge rather than as a personal affront. In part, gaining access to the news media requires developing a better understanding of the needs of news professionals. Trying to appreciate their perspectives, their limits, and their needs to respond to their audience is essential for building a constructive relationship with news professionals.

> **Rule 3:**
> *Understand the conventions and values that drive journalists.*

There are many theories regarding how news story selection takes place.[2] For our purposes, it is useful to think of four overlapping perspectives on how news becomes news. First, news comes from natural or spontaneous events, such as ① notable personal achievements, fires, murders, weather, traffic crashes, labor strikes, and the whole range of events that affect people or stimulate their interest.

Second, there is an extensive series of constructed events, such as news ② conferences, news releases, and staged events, that are used every day as a means for gaining access. This could involve releasing a report focusing on the financial contributions of the tobacco industry to Congress members' campaigns, holding a demonstration to protest the repeal of safety regulations in the workplace, or introducing a new policy initiative.

The third view of what constitutes news focuses on the personal interests ③ of journalists. The background, experiences, and views of the journalist serve as a filter through which professional judgments about news values are made. For example, one assignment editor who had recently had a baby was very interested in a story being pitched about the way some hospital delivery rooms push infant formula on new mothers, even though doing so may discourage breast-feeding, a healthier option. The assignment editor recalled seeing those formula packages in the hospital and wondering about the story behind them. On the other hand, she noted that if the story had been pitched to the afternoon assignment editor, a retired police officer, he might not have been as interested.

The first person the story has to be interesting to is the person who decides to cover it. The journalist—or editor who assigns the story—has to care about it or believe that someone in the audience will care about it. When presented with a story idea, news workers ask themselves, "Do I care?" If they care, logic allows them to assume that others in the audience would also care and to select stories on that basis. This way, they believe they can anticipate what their audience will respond to by paying attention to their own responses. As one network bureau chief explained, "I like to think that anything that interests me will probably interest everybody."[3]

When presented ③
with a story idea,
news workers ask
themselves, "Do I
care?"

An assignment editor we know says she is always interested in what she calls "water cooler stories"—things everyone will be talking about the next day around the office. These are stories that everyone can relate to and find interesting, whether or not they have an immediate impact on their lives— from White House sex scandals to an increase in the gasoline tax to the changing price of a cup of coffee.

The fourth view of how news gets selected focuses on the routine practices ④ or "beats" of news operations. The White House, city hall, crime, education, health, and the economy are all beats that are covered in the routine practice of the news. However, with budgetary and time constraints increasing in almost all newsrooms, fewer news organizations can afford the luxury of having reporters assigned to specialized beats; if nothing is happening in the health world one day, the health beat reporter is an unused asset. Instead, newsrooms, especially TV stations, are increasingly relying on general assignment reporters. This means a reporter may have little background on each story, knowing only what he or she can gather in a day or two before completing the story. (For advocates, this may mean developing relationships with a wider range of journalists; you can't afford to rely only on those covering your issue's beat.)

Other factors that influence which news stories are selected include the following:

Logistics

Simple concerns such as parking and easy access to news sites might influence whether a story is done, especially if there are competing stories. For instance, a violence prevention group planned a news conference at a cemetery outside of town; one TV reporter told the group that she would not likely cover the story because she could not get there and back in time for the broadcast. An assignment editor might choose which story to do based on which is easiest to do. Therefore, advocates should consider logistics from the journalist's point of view when creating news events.

Timing

News is immediate. The best stories are those still in progress. The urgency that characterizes a newsroom exists because everyone is eager to get the latest information on any story so it is as current as possible and relevant to today. Newsrooms receive a surprising number of calls from people pitching stories that happened yesterday. Unless there is significant interest and new information in the follow-up story, yesterday's news is not going to be covered today.

Serendipity

Serendipity plays a role in story selection because communication is not systematic in the newsroom. Inside the newsroom and out, it is whom you know, whom you talk to, and what your personal interests are that guide what is selected and what is included in a story. Although a distinct management hierarchy is responsible for final decisions about what is included in the news, anyone in the newsroom can and does pitch stories to anyone else.[4] The chaotic way information travels in newsrooms means it is useful to have many contacts at one outlet and to deliver your information in a variety of ways to several people at the same outlet.

How Can You Get Attention for Your Story?

Of course, your stories are important, or you wouldn't be working on them. But journalists can't possibly cover every important story every day. They only have a 22-minute news broadcast, or a limited number of column inches in a newspaper, or a few minutes at a time on the radio in which to tell the news that will appeal to the widest possible audience. So to get journalists' attention, you have to tell them about your stories and emphasize what's interesting about them.

Overall, pitch stories, not issues. A reporter is far more likely to do a story on a family struggling to find child care in your town than on the lack of affordable child care in general. Your goal may ultimately be to focus on issues, but to achieve that, you have to develop compelling stories, and compelling stories are specific, not general.

Rule 4:
Pitch stories, not issues.

There are some clear guidelines about what makes a story newsworthy—that is, interesting enough to be in the news. To get journalists' attention and convince them to cover your issues, media advocates have to structure stories so they fit the traditional patterns of newsworthiness. This means highlighting the aspects of your story that contain some of the following typical story elements. The more newsworthy elements your story contains and the broader the audience it interests, the more likely it will be to capture a reporter's attention.

Controversy and Conflict

Elements of Newsworthiness

Fights are common topics for news stories. The conflict might be between politicians, political parties, or council members and constituents. There is likely to be some controversy in most of the issues a media advocate works on—after all, if no one objects to the policy being proposed, then there is probably no need for a media advocacy strategy. But if, as is likely, there is opposition to what your group wants to do, what is it? How would you describe it to a journalist? Think about the story line, the plot and characters: Are there adversaries or other tensions in the story? Progressive advocates benefit from the fact that the conflict on their issues is often tantalizingly framed in what Simon Chapman calls "one of the most enduring themes in public health advocacy: the David and Goliath struggles of small, ill-equipped community groups representing issues of social justice against the giant and wealthy behemoths in industry or government."[5] This is an inherently news-worthy frame for your stories.

ADVOCACY IN ACTION: Henry Horner Mothers

A group of mothers who lived in the Henry Horner Homes, a notorious public housing project in Chicago, were fed up with the unsafe, unsanitary living conditions of the Homes: Elevators did not work, windows and light fixtures were broken, halls were graffiti-covered, and apartments were roach-infested. After meeting unsuccessfully with representatives of the Chicago Housing Authority (CHA) to ask for improved maintenance and basic repairs, the group mobilized to call media attention to the issue. With the help of the Chicago Video Project, they created a video news release showing the terrible conditions of the buildings and released it on the day they filed suit against the CHA in an attempt to have it "held to the same legal responsibilities and standards as other Chicago landlords."[6] In her comments during their press conference, spokeswoman Maureen Woodson said the CHA's promises to improve conditions had been broken too often: "Everything around us is broken. We are tired of broken promises and we are ready to fight all the way."[7] The abundant news coverage of the story reflected the theme of conflict between the sympathetic mothers and the powerful bureaucracy that had failed them.

Broad Interest

Ultimately, producing news is a business. That means, besides telling stories, the main objective is attracting the largest audience possible. The larger the number of people to whom a story is deemed meaningful, the more likely it will be covered. A large audience means higher revenues for the news outlet because it can charge more for advertising. News workers ask themselves: Does this affect a lot of people? What information do we have or can we get that will be important or interesting to the largest possible audience? From an advocate's perspective, appealing to broad interest means articulating those aspects of the issue that most of the audience would be concerned about, affected by, or interested in. Does your story affect a lot of people, or does it relate to groups of special concern such as children?

For example, according to the research department at one local TV news station, stay-at-home moms watch the news at 5 p.m. They care about their children, so stories about young children are likely to be aired in the 5 o'clock newscast.[8]

ADVOCACY IN ACTION: Phone Books and Rain Forests

Environmental advocates concerned about the destruction of ancient rain forests found a way to make their issue relevant to large numbers of people: They asked the local phone company to stop printing phone books on paper made from rain forest lumber. The proposal took the form of a shareholder resolution, thus capturing the interest of business reporters and business people, as well as environmental reporters and environmentalists. Advocates argued that by taking steps to preserve the rain forest, the phone company could actually attract more customers in the environmentally conscious Northern California region, thereby benefiting both the environment and the company. As a representative of the coalition said, "We're asking stockholders to vote for saving the last great North American rain forests. In today's deregulated telephone markets, a vote for the environment is a vote for the company's bottom line."[9]

Injustice

Exposing the consequences of an agency's or person's action is a favorite topic for news. Are there basic inequalities or unfair circumstances that your story illustrates? How did the injustice occur? Who is responsible for fixing it? Injustice stories really address the audience's acute sense of fairness—anything that makes the audience say, "That's not right; somebody should do something about that."

ADVOCACY IN ACTION: Hungry Kids Versus Bureaucrats

A nutrition advocate pitched a story to a TV news assignment editor about a school breakfast program that had been funded by the state; school districts could automatically qualify for the program and provide free breakfasts to needy children, but some districts had failed to set up the program due to bureaucratic red tape. The editor immediately responded, "You're telling me kids are going hungry and they don't have to? I'll cover it." She knew that the injustice of hungry kids was enough to automatically make that story newsworthy; the opportunity to expose bureaucratic ineptitude and the ability to show visuals of children made it even more appealing.

Irony

An ironic story describes a dramatic contradiction that halts readers in their tracks. What is ironic or unusual about your story? Is there something unexpected that makes this situation different from others?

ADVOCACY IN ACTION: Economic Trends in Sonoma County

A group of family advocates in Sonoma County, California, was preparing a report showing that one fifth of the county's families did not make enough money to cover their basic needs—shelter, food, utilities, child care, and transportation. The group had a series of proposals to help struggling families become economically self-sufficient but were having trouble attracting media attention to the issue. Then, a major business group convened a conference on the county's "economic vitality," touting the area's booming business climate. In the wake of the headlines on the area's economic vitality, the advocates were able to bring media attention to the ironic reality that, in fact, one in five families was struggling to make ends meet.

Local Peg

Except for the networks, most news is local. Even networks need a local example to illustrate the issue of national interest. Making national stories relevant to local audiences is a primary goal of most local news outlets. What about your story is important or meaningful to the local audience that buys the paper or watches the news? If something is going on nationally that is important to your issue, how does it translate in your town? How can you illustrate that connection for reporters?

ADVOCACY IN ACTION: Hands Off Halloween

The national Hands Off Halloween campaign aims to convince beer makers not to use icons of the children's holiday—pumpkins, witches, ghouls, and goblins—to sell alcohol. Across the country, local alcohol control advocates generated coverage in their local news by holding media events at local grocery stores and calling on local merchants to refuse to display Halloween-theme beer promotions. The local angle on a national effort made the story more newsworthy for local media outlets.

Personal Angle

Most journalists seek a personal story through which to tell the news. They look for that typical case, someone who can embody the issue so audiences can empathize with the person and feel concern for the problem.

Human interest means stories that evoke tenderness, compassion, humor, or other positive human qualities. People care about the subjects of these stories because they care about the condition of humanity. Are there people with direct experience with the issue who can provide an authentic voice in your story? Are they willing to speak to a reporter, and have they been adequately prepared?

ADVOCACY IN ACTION: "It could happen to anyone; It happened to me."

When a driver running a red light hit pedestrians Curtis Kerry and James Brennan, it focused an entire city's attention on the problem of pedestrian safety. Kerry was one of nearly 30 people killed in San Francisco each year in red light-running collisions. Brennan was severely injured; his left leg was crushed, and his pelvis and shoulder broken, requiring months of physical therapy. Ironically, before the incident, Brennan was a volunteer at the Trauma Foundation, which works to prevent traffic injuries; this connection gave him the outlet he needed to turn his personal experience into a crusade. His proposed solutions: Make stoplights and street signs bigger, remove signs cluttering intersections, and prosecute red light-running as a crime. The dramatic story of the crash and his painful recovery attracted news attention with a compelling personal story; he then had the access he needed to work for the changes he wanted to see happen to make streets safer for pedestrians.

Breakthrough

A breakthrough is something that happens for the first time, an indication that from here on, things will never be the same. Especially in science and medical news, if reporters can say that this is the first time something has happened, or this new information answers questions we've never been able to answer before, they are eager to tell the story. (The unfortunate consequence of this desire among news professionals is that the normally incremental process in scientific and medical research gets distorted: "breakthroughs" are reported when none are there.) If something is new or different about your story, be sure to inform the journalist about what it is and why it is important. Does your story mark an important historical "first" or other milestone? Is there evidence of change that can be highlighted?

There are various ways to think about how to use breakthroughs to increase the newsworthiness of your issue. Typically, people think about medical or technological breakthroughs, such as new cancer treatments or a faster computer. However, there are social and political breakthroughs, as well. For example, when tobacco executives admitted for the first time that nicotine was addictive, this was a breakthrough because it had never happened before. When women or people of color break a barrier to make them the first to win an award, to be elected, or to have a certain kind of job, this is usually seen as a breakthrough. During labor strikes, the concept of breakthrough is applied when there is an event that changes the bargaining process, such as when management agrees to withdraw benefit reductions from the table. The challenge for your group is to think about your issue and identify the different kinds of breakthroughs that might be useful.

ADVOCACY IN ACTION: A Community Comes Together[10]

In the Williamsburg community of Brooklyn, New York, the city decided to build an incinerator that would burn 3,000 tons of trash daily. The community was primarily populated by ultra orthodox Jews and Latinos—two groups with a long history of mistrust and antagonistic relations in the neighborhood. The groups joined together under the common interest of protecting children and maintained a delicate coalition to work against the incinerator proposal. Author Randy Shaw explained, "The willingness of two completely distinct groups who distrusted each other and fought over many issues to join forces against the incinerator sent a powerful message throughout the state."[11] This breakthrough added power to the incinerator opposition and increased the newsworthiness of the coalition's public events, such as marches and rallies. One of the events in the decade-long struggle was a march including Hasidim, African Americans, and Latinos on the eve of Martin Luther King's birthday. Shaw quotes a leader from the Latino community: "We are marching for unity and in light of the racial tension that has a hold of the city, we will demonstrate, different ethnic groups together, in a show of outrage."[12] According to Shaw, "*The New York Times'* photo of the march was captioned, 'Environmental concerns unite a neighborhood.' "

Anniversary

Anniversaries, or milestones, are markers of progress or time passed since a noteworthy event. News organizations are fond of using time markers as a reason to retell a story or reexamine an issue after some time has passed. Anniversaries are made salient by their history as news events: President

Kennedy's assassination; the space shuttle *Challenger's* explosion; the Oklahoma City bombing; major earthquakes, fires, floods, and other natural disasters. Anniversaries can be a useful device to examine the effects of a policy six months or a year after it is implemented. What news or other events can you link to your issue? How long has it been—six months, a year—since a key news event happened? How can your story be associated with a local, national, or topical historical event?

ADVOCACY IN ACTION: Golden Gate Bridge

More people have committed suicide at the Golden Gate Bridge—by jumping off—than at any other location in the world. All other high-profile suicide sites now have physical barriers that have successfully prevented deaths. A San Francisco Bay Area coalition formed to advocate for the construction of a suicide barrier that could prevent virtually all of the 20 to 40 known suicides at the bridge each year. Research has shown that people deterred from jumping from the bridge tend not to commit suicide by other means.

To increase the visibility of this issue and communicate a sense of urgency to the Golden Gate Bridge District Board, the coalition decided to take advantage of the 60th anniversary of the opening of the Golden Gate Bridge. They knew that the media would be running stories about the beauty and majesty of this landmark recognized around the world. The coalition called a press conference to highlight "the dark side" of the bridge and call for a suicide barrier as a solution.

By using the anniversary as a hook, the news conference received significant coverage. One television station ran a long story showing the barrier model and highlighting the arguments of the coalition. In just a few days, the coalition was contacted by the chief engineer of the bridge district—their target—to find out more about the model developed by the engineering students. As one coalition member noted, "We stole the birthday from the Golden Gate Bridge." They used the opportunity to advance the need for a suicide barrier and establish the coalition as a major player.

Seasonal Peg

Because news organizations want the largest audience they can find, they try to find stories on topics that affect everyone. The seasons, and holidays, affect a broad audience: Everyone knows when it is New Year's Eve. At the same time, journalists are tired of telling the same story again and again. Every year, in all sections of the newspaper and on broadcast news, reporters and editors do stories related to winter cold and summer heat; there are Back to School stories at the beginning of September, Mother's Day family stories, New Year's Eve and high school graduation drinking and driving stories, Halloween giant pumpkin stories, Thanksgiving hunger stories, and Christmas charity stories. Each of these times presents an opportunity for new angles on old stories if you can connect your issue for the reporter. How can your story be attached to a holiday or seasonal event?

ADVOCACY IN ACTION: Buy Nothing Day

Around the world, advocates concerned with the effects of overconsumption join together in an annual "Buy Nothing Day," a 24-hour moratorium on consumer spending. On Buy Nothing Day, participants call attention to the environmental, physical, and psychological effects of rampant consumerism, with events including street theater and "cut up your credit card" booths in local malls. Kalle Lasn, founder of the Vancouver, B.C.-based Media Foundation, which initiated Buy Nothing Day, made a strategic decision to hold the event on what is typically the biggest shopping day of the year: the day after Thanksgiving in the United States.[13] This seasonal link gives reporters a timely new angle on the holiday shopping frenzy and helps attract attention to the group's issue.

Celebrity

Much has been written about the media's attention to celebrities, which reached a heightened frenzy after Princess Diana was killed in a car crash. A celebrity might attract news attention to your issue because celebrities appeal to a large audience. A celebrity does not have to be a movie star or a national figure; a local resident with special renown can attract attention, as well. Celebrities are no guarantee of attention, and it is important to be sure of what the celebrity will say, as with any public representative. Is there a celebrity already involved with or willing to lend his or her name to your issue? Or, is a celebrity involved on the opposite side of your issue, so that you could attract news attention by making him or her part of your target?

ADVOCACY IN ACTION: Celebrity Sweatshops

Advocates working on international labor issues know how linking a celebrity to their cause can boost its newsworthiness. In April 1996, labor advocate Charles Kernaghan told a congressional committee that celebrity Kathie Lee Gifford's signature line of Wal-Mart sportswear was made in a Honduran factory "where 15-year-old girls earn 31 cents an hour and work 75-hour weeks."[14] Gifford responded emotionally to the charges on her talk show, with the effect of extending the media coverage. By the time Gifford ultimately joined New York Governor George Pataki and others in trying to ban the sale of apparel made in sweatshops, public attention was focused on the issue as never before. As Kernaghan told *The New York Times* about his strategy of attracting media interest by targeting celebrity product endorsers, "Their image is everything. They live or die by their image. That gives you a certain power over them."

Other celebrities have been linked to the issue in creative ways, as noted by David Korten: "The $20 million that basketball star Michael Jordan reportedly received in 1992 for promoting Nike shoes exceeded the entire annual payroll of the Indonesian factories that made them."[15]

Visuals

Pictures, especially moving pictures, hold an exalted place on television news. Without visuals, the story might not get told. "In TV," said one producer, "video dominates. Words define, shape, reference the pictures. But it's really the pictures that tell the story."[16] An exciting visual can increase the likelihood a story will be done. Even though viewers may have read about the story in the paper or heard it on the radio, the local evening news is the first time they will see it. For TV news, to a large extent, story selection is determined by who has video or who can get it. On the assignment desk in one local TV newsroom, the assignment editor would respond to story pitches by asking, "What would we see if we went there?"[17] What creative and interesting visuals can you provide with your story?

ADVOCACY IN ACTION: The Baby Brigade

A group of children's advocates was concerned about the lack of affordable, high-quality child care. They assembled a "baby brigade" to gather at city hall in San Francisco to stress the need for the mayor to increase budget allocations for subsidized care. They deliberately chose to create a carnival-like atmosphere, with clowns, balloons, music, and lots of cute babies and children. The result was a wonderful, lively scene that provided great visuals, resulting in extensive coverage from three local TV stations and the two largest newspapers.

Bear in mind that at least two people have to want to do the story: the reporter and the reporter's editor. Even if the journalist is very eager to work with you, she or he will still have to convince an editor that the piece is worth including with the rest of the day's news—and that may mean convincing an editor why your story should be done instead of the one a coworker is pitching. The more information you can give the reporter to show that your story is newsworthy, the better he or she will be able to make the case to do your story.

Summary

Our third rule is: Understand the conventions and rules that drive journalists. Journalists are professionals who must adhere to a set of standards. If you want to work effectively with them, you must know and respect these standards. The more elements of newsworthiness your story includes, the more likely it is to be reported.

Our fourth rule is: Pitch stories, not issues. It is difficult for journalists, particularly broadcast journalists, to get a handle on the broad issues that advocates are trying to address. In gaining access to the media, think in terms of specific stories that can ultimately shed light on the larger issue and advance your particular solution.

Checklist: What Makes Your Story Newsworthy?

The more newsworthy elements your story contains and the broader the audience it interests, the more likely it will show up on the evening news or in the newspaper.

Controversy/conflict	Are there adversaries or other tensions in the story?
Broad interest	Does this story affect a lot of people, or does it relate to groups of special concern such as children?
Injustice	Are there basic inequalities or unfair circumstances?
Irony	What is ironic or unusual about this story? Is there hypocrisy to reveal?
Local peg	Why is this story important or meaningful to local residents?
Personal angle	Is there a person with direct experience with the issue who can provide an authentic voice in the story? (Make sure such people are trained advocates as well as traditional "victims.")
Breakthrough	Does this story mark an important historical "first" or other event?
Anniversary peg	Can this story be linked to the anniversary of a local, national, or topical historical milestone?
Seasonal peg	Can this story be attached to a holiday or seasonal event?
Celebrity	Is there a celebrity already involved with or willing to lend his or her name to the issue?
Visuals	What interesting visuals can you create or take advantage of to give journalists something interesting to shoot?

Getting the attention of the media, we have found, is relatively easy. The real challenge is to shape the story from a solution-oriented policy perspective rather than the personal individual perspective that is so ingrained in the conventional news formula. We now turn our attention to this issue of framing.

Notes _____

1. Lippmann, W. (1922). *Public opinion.* New York: Free Press, p. 214.

2. Gans, H. (1979). *Deciding what's news.* New York: Vintage Books.

3. Dorfman, L. (1994). *News operations: How television reports on health.* Doctoral dissertation, University of California at Berkeley.

4. Dorfman, 1994.

5. Chapman, S., & Lupton, D. (1994). *The fight for public health: Principles and practice of media advocacy.* London: BMJ Publishing Group, p. x.

6. Henry Horner Mother's Guild Video News Release, 1991.

7. Maureen Woodson, local Chicago TV news coverage, May 31, 1991.

8. Dorfman, 1994.

9. Pelline, J. (1996, September 10). PacBell's phone books become shareholder issue. *San Francisco Chronicle,* p. B1.

10. Summarized from Shaw, R. (1996). *The activist's handbook: A primer for the 1990s and beyond.* Berkeley: University of California Press.

11. Shaw, 1996, p. 96

12. Shaw, 1996, p. 96.

13. Berner, R. (1997, November 19). A holiday greeting networks won't air: Shoppers are "pigs." *The Wall Street Journal,* p. A1.

14. Greenhouse, S. (1996, June 18). A crusader makes celebrities tremble. *New York Times,* p. B4.

15. Korten, D. (1995). *When corporations rule the world.* West Hartford, CT: Kumarian Press.

16. Dorfman, 1994.

17. Dorfman, 1994.

4

THINKING LIKE AN ADVOCATE
Shaping the Story

———————— ◆ ————————

It is not enough for a ~~movement~~ to have logic or justice or even millions of people on its side; it has to be able to tell powerful stories.

Professor Fred Block, University of California, Davis

———————— ————————

Getting your story into the news is only half of the challenge. It is critical *how* your issue is covered, not just whether it is covered. Framing is the process that moves advocates from the basic consideration of the presence or absence of an issue to how that issue is portrayed.

As Gerald Kosicki points out, "Media 'gatekeepers' do not merely keep watch over information, shuffling it here and there. Instead, they engage in active construction of the messages, emphasizing certain aspects of an issue and not others."[1] Advocates need to understand that the way journalists shape news stories influences what viewers and readers think about the issue and its possible solutions.

What Is Framing?

Frames are the boundaries around a news story; they delineate what is and is not news. Just as you make decisions, some conscious, some instinctive, whenever you shoot a snapshot, so journalists decide, sometimes consciously, sometimes formulaically, what to include in a story. Because everything can't be told in each story, journalists must make selections. Thus, framing is our practical name for the selection process a journalist goes through when deciding what issues, ideas, images, and other elements should be included in the news story.[2] The news frame draws attention to specific parts of the story, relegates other elements to the background, and leaves some aspects out entirely.

Framing can also refer to the attitude or perspective included in the story. This is commonly considered the "angle" or "spin" on the story. Understanding frames in this way means paying attention to the symbols, metaphors, or visuals that evoke a particular meaning. For instance, Charlotte Ryan identified the range of metaphors in press coverage on labor unions: unions as the small David fighting the Goliath of big business, unions as troublemakers, or unions as corrupt "fat cat" bureaucracies. The symbols in these frames served to depict unions as positive forces serving the cause of justice and protecting the worker or, conversely, as a corrupt bureaucracy sapping energy from the worker.[3]

Why Are News Frames Important to Advocates?

The way issues are framed helps news consumers decide who is responsible for the cause and solution of a problem. For example, media effects research shows that TV news viewers typically will attribute responsibility for fixing the problem to the people with the problem.[4] The dominant frame in TV news emphasizes isolated events or people and minimizes the larger social and physical landscape.

Consider two ABC news stories broadcast on the same night in 1996. The first was a story about "crumbling schools and no money to fix them" across the nation, complete with pictures of dilapidated buildings, leaky auditoriums, and abandoned classrooms. The story was framed in terms of institutional responsibilities to serve children in education: a social accountability frame. The onus was put on government to fix the problem.

This was followed by a "Person of the Week" feature about Camera Barret, "the valedictorian who had no home," a teen who, despite being homeless because of running away after a violent argument with his mother, became valedictorian of his high school class. He "had all the excuses in the world" not to excel, as the correspondent put it, yet he did, winning a $16,000 scholarship to Cornell University. In this story, individual achievement trumps social justice concerns. There is no attention paid to ameliorating the terrible conditions that affected Camera Barret (and thousands of youth like him). Instead, the focus is on Barret's exceptional commitment and abilities, conveyed with images such as Barret doing his homework while riding the city bus. Barret's is the typical news frame—the great heart-tugging story of the triumphant individual who beats daunting odds, the "young man who proved that persistence pays."

The problem is that the second story virtually negates the first, an important story about crumbling schools. It begs the question of whether it is really important to fix the schools when, as Barret's story proves, even kids facing the worst conditions can succeed if they have the desire and work really hard.

The constant struggle between these two frames, institutional accountability and personal responsibility, is regularly reflected in the news. Most often the news covers the compelling personal story about an individual who overcomes adversity; this type of story reassures viewers that the system works when people work hard enough. Because our individual-oriented culture is reflected in the majority of news stories, audiences will usually identify personal responsibility as the solution unless they are presented with equally compelling information that makes them consider broader factors.

The challenge of articulating the policy frame lies in the fact that the progressive values in advocacy stories often tend to run counter to the frames of individualism and the free market that are so dominant in U.S. culture and media. Your arguments may not automatically resonate with the prevailing values the way those on the other side do. This means that whereas your opposition can often get by with merely *asserting* something to be true, you must spend more effort *explaining* why your position is true. For example, alcohol companies can assert that restrictions on advertising are a violation of the right to free speech, whereas health advocates have to explain that the Supreme Court has ruled that commercial speech can be restricted in certain circumstances and that, in this circumstance, the greater public good is served. You can see why advocates have their work cut out for them.

Of course, the way the news reinforces individualism is often doubly frustrating for advocates because they feel they have no control over it. And that's true: You cannot control what the reporter says or how he or she shapes the story. You can only control what you say to the reporter, what materials you provide, what sources you refer him or her to, what facts you focus on, what stories you tell. By describing ways in which you can "shape the story," we do not mean to imply that you literally have the ability to determine what is included in the story and what is not. But you *can* be creative in supplying journalists with story elements that illustrate the solution you support.

How Can Advocates Frame Their News Stories to Support Policy Change?

Rule 5:
*Supply journalists with creative story elements
that illustrate the solution you support.*

Fortunately, there are several concrete steps you can take in planning media work to help make the progressive perspective resonate in stories on your issue:

Translate the individual problem into a social issue

Advocates routinely try to show that the problems they address, far from being only matters of personal behavior, are in fact caused in part by broader social forces. The problem of cigarette smoking, for instance, becomes the larger issue of the "single greatest preventable cause of death in the United States." Advocates trying to get a suicide barrier erected on the Golden Gate Bridge talk about the last suicide icon in the world without a barrier. In these cases, and others, the challenge is to counter the dominant public sentiment that whether you smoke, commit suicide, consume alcohol, or partake in any other form of "self-destructive" behavior, you are making a personal choice. If the problem continues to be perceived exclusively as a personal concern, there is no need for social action, only increased awareness and personal education.

To shift this frame, emphasize social problems and broader contributing causes in addition to individual choices. This means, in a very basic way, talking about policies, not behavior. Policies sought may be legislative, but they need not be: A policy could be as simple as getting healthy snacks placed in high school cafeteria vending machines or as comprehensive as requiring air bags in all new automobiles. The change in language from *smoking* to *tobacco* demonstrates the shift from behavior to policies. Smoking is an act performed by an individual; tobacco is a product that is manufactured, marketed, and regulated. Shifting language lays the groundwork to help journalists and their audiences understand the importance of addressing solutions that go beyond individual action. If tobacco is a social issue, it is appropriate to make rules about it that everyone in society must respect.

Assign primary responsibility

Remember that most news consumers, unless given additional information, will assume that the person with the problem is responsible for solving it. Even the most sympathetic portrait of a struggling mom on welfare tends to lead audiences to suggest that the solution is for her to try harder to find a job or get help from family and friends.[5] To help audiences to understand the social perspective on problems, you must constantly assert the corporate, governmental, or institutional responsibility for the problem. Name the individual or body whom you hold responsible for taking action. For instance, violence prevention advocates focus on the widespread availability of cheap, poorly designed handguns rather than succumbing to the personal portrait of youth as "teen predators." It doesn't mean they absolve anyone of heinous acts, but it does mean they also hold manufacturers and legislators responsible for the lethality and availability of the weapons.

When talking to journalists about responsibility, progressives can emphasize one of their core values: social justice. Those with the least power, those who are marginalized because of historical discrimination, disproportionately bear the burden of hazardous exposure of all kinds. For instance, there is basic injustice when communities of color are used as toxic dumping grounds, suffering the most from pollution and benefiting the least from cleanup programs. To treat this as an issue of social justice rather than just a problem of the free market elevates the discussion to a higher level; it adds moral authority and political pressure to the issue. As the Rev. Benjamin Chavis, Jr., said, "The idea of civil rights is expanding to include freedom from pollution, and an emphasis on social justice is being added to the idea of environmental protection."[6] With this language, Chavis defines the problem as no longer merely personal but one of how hazards are allocated in American society; it is a question of justice.

However, merely saying something is a social justice issue has limited persuasive power per se. To convey the issue of fairness, develop a story that personalizes the injustice and then provide a clear picture of who is benefiting from the condition. It becomes a story about the exploiter and exploited; the focus shifts from the victim to the victimizer. Tobacco control advocates have been very effective in creating stories showing powerful tobacco company executives exploiting children and youth for profit. The key to advancing the social justice and fairness issue is to create a story that leads people to say, "That just isn't right. There ought to be a law to do something about that."

> *The key to advancing the social justice and fairness issue is to create a story that leads people to say, "That just isn't right."*

Present a solution

As we noted in Chapter 1, journalists will always ask some version of two questions: What is the problem, and what is the solution you propose? The first question is fairly easy. Research often provides abundant data, reports, and books that describe the problem in great detail; who it happens to; its distribution in the population according to age, gender, region, race, and ethnicity; its effects and anticipated outcomes. Most advocates can speak volumes about the problem.

Where people often struggle is in answering the second question. Without a clear solution to advance, getting media attention to your problem may actually be counterproductive: You may have raised concern about the issue without giving people a specific solution to consider. This is why we recommend that you usually should not attempt to get media coverage unless you have a specific, concrete policy solution to offer.

In fact, advocates often seem to spend 90% of their time talking about the problem and 10% focusing on the solution. Sometimes this is necessary: For instance, tobacco control advocates spent decades trying to expose the industry's deceptive practices before the political environment could support any serious policy solutions. In many cases, however, the problem is well understood, and your challenge should be to focus more on what you want to have happen. Keep track of how much you talk with reporters about the problem and how much you talk about the solution. Check your sound bites, quotes, and the overall composition of the stories to see whether they are primarily "ain't it awful" stories or "change is possible" stories.

ADVOCACY IN ACTION: Have a Clear Solution

• A disability rights group was trying to increase the proportion of the Medicare budget spent on supporting independent living, rather than nursing home care. This enormously complicated issue was effectively communicated by saying, "We want 25% of the Medicare budget shifted from nursing homes to attendant care." Thus, a highly complex problem was given a clear, concise solution. The advocates knew what they wanted and they said it—so succinctly that their line was often repeated by reporters in the extensive news coverage they generated.

• The Coalition for a Suicide Barrier on the Golden Gate Bridge included their solution in their name. They also sponsored a contest in an engineering class at the University of California at Berkeley that resulted in a scale model showing what the bridge would look like with the barrier. They literally made their solution visible.

• In more than 40 communities in California, people were fed up with high rates of handgun violence. They decided they wanted to reduce the availability of the cheap, easy-to-conceal handguns that were involved in many youth homicides. They introduced various kinds of ordinances in their city councils that banned the sale of junk guns or Saturday night specials.

When describing your solution, do not list every possible solution; highlight the one your group has given top priority, the one that most needs to be advanced *today*. This means knowing what you want to say and being able to say it simply. Practice with colleagues until the answers roll off your tongue. Effective advocates can offer a compelling statement about their problem *and* the solution in 10 to 12 seconds; that should be your goal as well.

Make a practical appeal

It's critical to emphasize the ways in which your solution is a winner from a practical as well as moral perspective. Policy is important from a practical perspective because it is a more effective means for changing behavior than education alone; it changes the conditions that generated the problem in the first place. Appeals generally must emphasize that your proposed policy can save lives, save money, protect children or other "innocents," provide a fair chance, increase opportunity, or right an injustice. It is also important that your appeals invoke shared values—independence, self-sufficiency, self-determination, freedom, protection from outside harms. Have concrete examples of how your policy will be of benefit to the entire community—not only those who suffer from the problem.

- Disability rights advocates pointed out that by allowing people to stay in their homes rather than being placed in nursing homes, money could be saved and people with disabilities could become more independent, productive members of society.
- The suicide prevention coalition explained to people that "Suicide is a permanent solution to a temporary problem" and emphasized that a barrier would give people a second chance.
- Advocates to limit availability of guns argued that having a handgun in the home, rather than being a protective factor, was actually a risk factor increasing the likelihood of death or injury to a family member.

Develop story elements

The challenge in trying to influence a story's frame is that the journalists, not you, control what is included and excluded in a story. But if you understand the business of news reporting and can anticipate journalists' needs, you can offer story elements that will make it much easier for the reporter to include your perspective as part of the story. These include:

Use compelling visuals and symbols

TV news in particular must have good visuals. In fact, TV news workers often collect *pictures* as opposed to *news*; they illustrate stories that may already be in print.[7] Dramatic visuals can create a story, compelling journalists to cover what they might otherwise have overlooked.

For example, disability rights activist Paul Longmore was frustrated by an unjust bureaucracy that prevented him from earning even modest royalties on a book he wrote; if he made even $300 per year, he would lose his Supplemental Security Income benefits and, more important, the subsidized medical insurance that helped pay for essential in-home care. After working for change within the system, his frustration drove him to seek media attention. But the issue was a challenge to make newsworthy: "I mean, what was I gonna do to get publicity?" Longmore said. "Disability rights activists had been trying for years to get news media coverage of what is a very complicated and very dull issue."[8]

As a newsworthy protest, Longmore decided to burn his own book, thinking it "would be a dramatic symbol." When his biography of George Washington went up in flames in front of the Social Security Administration building, it did indeed attract news attention—a prominent story on the front page of the *Los Angeles Times*. Longmore credits this coverage with helping advance a congressional amendment correcting some of the injustices he was protesting, which passed a few months later.

It is important to think about the visuals of your story even if you are seeking print coverage. Newspapers are giving more prominence to photographs and graphics. Plus, if you can bring a vivid picture to mind with your story, you will have an easier time convincing journalists of its news value. For instance, a teenager bought a pack of cigarettes from a vending machine in the basement of a House of Representatives building while wearing a T-shirt that said, "I am 14 years old."[9] Although the newspaper that covered this story did not show a photo of the youth in the T-shirt, the teenager's action painted a picture; it used irony to draw attention to the problem of tobacco availability. Tobacco control groups used the news attention to highlight Congress's failure to combat the tobacco industry. The news story was effective because it easily brought a picture to mind, first for the journalist assigned to do the story and then for the journalist's readers.

A good visual is like a magnet and can be irresistible. It attracts the reporter and visually punctuates your point.

A good visual is like a magnet and can be irresistible. It attracts the reporter and, by doing so, visually punctuates your point. But don't get carried away. Make sure that your visual is more than cute or creative. You must assess it, no matter how wonderful you think it might be, as to whether it not only gets attention but also illustrates your point.

ADVOCACY IN ACTION: The Polar Bear and the Statue of Liberty

Use visuals to dramatically make or reinforce your key points in a compelling way:
   • In San Francisco, tenant activists were advocating for stronger heat laws because residential hotels for low-income people were, in some cases, heatless. When hearings were held before the County Board of Supervisors, a person dressed up as a polar bear handed out informational fliers.[10]
   • Tobacco control activists were concerned about the message that Philip Morris was sending in its cross-country tour of the Bill of Rights. The advocates constructed a model of the Statue of Liberty as an image that could visually and symbolically compete with the Bill of Rights. However, unlike the real statue, this one had a cigarette instead of a torch, and was shackled to a pack of cigarettes. Her base was constructed of cigarettes purchased by children and included a digital counter that displayed the number of people who had died of smoking-related causes from Philip Morris brands since the beginning of the tour.

Develop media bites

When you want your message to be in the news, you must work within the realistic constraints of news time. This means understanding that no matter how complicated your story is, or how much work you do with a reporter, or how long you spend being interviewed, chances are that only one or two of your sentences will make it into the final news piece. (And that's only if you are one of the most compelling spokespeople on the issue.) Therefore, your task is to plan in advance how to be as strategic as possible about those one or two sentences. Once you've decided *what* you want to

---

Checklist: Components of a Successful Media Bite

Keep it short and simple—15 seconds *maximum.*
Speak to shared values.
Talk about what is at stake.
Use reasonable language.
Use irony, if appropriate.
Evoke pictures.
Take a stand—present a solution.
Frame the problem and your proposed solution in terms of institutional accountability, rather than individual responsibility.

NOTE: Thanks to We Interrupt This Message, a media activism organization in San Francisco, for some of these pointers.

---

convey, then you figure out *how* to say it in a way that will make it more likely to be quoted.

Despite the complexity and depth of your issue, you must be prepared to make it come alive for news consumers in short **media bites.** Successful media bites often convey some irony, sometimes comparing your issue to another problem that people feel strongly about.

How do you come up with media bites? Practice with colleagues, trying out different ways to describe the problem and convey your solution. Start by trying out answers to typical questions about your issue. Speak to shared values, stressing themes such as fairness, common sense, or protection of children. Talk about what is at stake and who is affected. Explain what this will mean to people's lives. And don't be afraid to take a stand.

Here are some examples of effective media bites:

• **Keep it short and simple**—15 seconds maximum. That amounts to two to three sentences, tops, although one punchy sentence is even better.

> *Example:* "I'm tired of Cadillac prisons and jalopy schools."—California Superintendent of Education Delaine Eastin[11]

• **Speak to shared values.** Stress themes that matter to the majority of people, such as fairness, common sense, or protection of children. It is helpful if you can illustrate why the problem is one that everyone should care about, as opposed to one that only those who suffer from it should care about.

Example: "It is easy to think of smoking as an adult problem. It is adults who die from tobacco-related diseases. [But] . . . nicotine addiction begins when most tobacco users are teenagers, so let's call this what it really is: a pediatric disease."—FDA Commissioner David Kessler[12]

- **Talk about what is at stake.** Who is affected? What will this mean to people's lives?

  Example: "Too many kids are born into zip codes of shame. They live in a city glutted with guns, drugs, and alcohol. They plan more for their funerals than their futures."—California State Senator Tom Hayden[13]

- **Use reasonable language.** No matter how strong your position, articulate it in mainstream language. Don't use jargon or acronyms. technical

  Example: "Toys are subjected to strict safety measures . . . and yet in the gun industry, there is absolutely no regulation or standards of manufacture."—Sarah Brady, chair, Handgun Control Inc.[14]

- **Consider using irony.** Ironic comparisons between your issue or target and another issue with which the public is very familiar can underscore your message effectively. It can help highlight the absurdity of an assertion by your opposition.

  Example: "To say that unwed mothers cause poverty is like saying that hungry people cause famine or sick people cause disease."—Katha Pollitt[15]

- **Evoke pictures.** If you can make your audience see what you are talking about, your point is more memorable and has more impact.

  Example: "In my neighborhood, it's as easy for kids to get guns as school supplies."—Adina Medina, 18, Target Safe Neighborhoods member[16]

- **Take a stand—present a solution.** The best messages don't just describe the problem, they say what should be done about it.

  Example: The Golden Gate bridge is "the world's leading suicide landmark. . . . Putting a suicide barrier up would provide many, many people with a second chance."—UC Berkeley School of Public Health professor Lawrence Wallack[17]

- **Frame the problem and your proposed solution in terms of institutional accountability, rather than just individual responsibility.** Name the individual or body whom you hold responsible for taking action.

Example: "We hope that the lawsuit will make a difference; we hope it will result in [the Chicago Housing Authority] being held to the same standard that any other landlord in the city of Chicago is held to."—William Wilen, Legal Assistance Foundation[18]

Calculate social math[19]

Every day, people are bombarded with news stories involving very large numbers. We hear about billions of dollars for various programs and projects, or we might learn that hundreds of thousands of people are at risk for a particular disease, or that a large percentage of the population feel a certain way about a particular issue. We know the numbers are large, but more often than not we are numbed rather than informed because we simply don't have a way of understanding the meaning of the number.

Advocates must become skilled in translating large numbers so they become interesting to the journalist and meaningful to the audience. Social math is the practice of making large numbers comprehensible and compelling by placing them in a social context that provides meaning. There are several ways to do this:

- **Break down numbers by time.** For example, a new study comes out showing that 3 million teenagers are diagnosed with a sexually transmitted disease every year.[20] You can say that amounts to more than 8,200 teenagers a day or more than 340 an hour. You could even estimate conservatively that every weekend, more than 16,000 teenagers will be infected with an STD.

- **Break down numbers by place.** For example, research shows that every year, roughly 1 million youth start smoking[21]; this is about 2,700 children every day. You can say that this is the equivalent of more than 33,000 classrooms of students every year or 90 classrooms a day (assuming a class size of 30). You could also point out that this would be equivalent to all the youth in a specific city or cities in your area.

- **Provide comparisons with familiar things.** For example, in 1993, health care reform was high on the public agenda, and the Canadian single payer system was a potential model. Some in the United States were arguing that the Canadian system was not a good one and that Canadians really preferred a U.S. private insurance model. However, a poll found that only 3% of Canadians believed a U.S.-type system would be preferable. To drive this point home, one advocate noted, "To put that in perspective, 16% of Canadians believe that Elvis Presley is still alive."[22]

In another example, advocates concerned abut gun violence in California found that there were more than 11,000 gun dealers in the state in 1996. To put this in context, they created a chart showing the number of gun dealers in comparison to the state's McDonald's (850), high schools (2,170), and libraries (1,024). (See Figure 4.1.) This brought the issue of gun availability

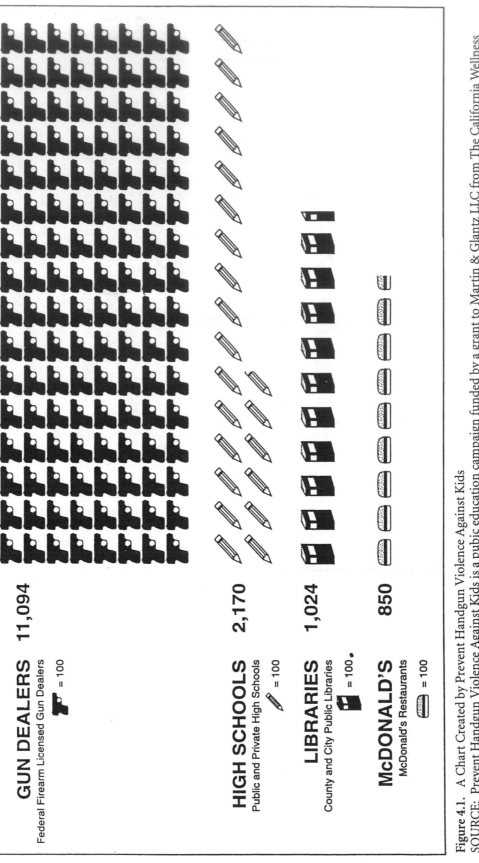

State of California
Gun Dealer Comparisons

GUN DEALERS 11,094
Federal Firearm Licensed Gun Dealers
= 100

HIGH SCHOOLS 2,170
Public and Private High Schools
= 100

LIBRARIES 1,024
County and City Public Libraries
= 100.

McDONALD'S 850
McDonald's Restaurants
= 100

Figure 4.1. A Chart Created by Prevent Handgun Violence Against Kids
SOURCE: Prevent Handgun Violence Against Kids is a pubic education campaign funded by a grant to Martin & Glantz LLC from The California Wellness Foundation. All statistics are for the State of California. Data on gun dealers: Bureau of Alcohol, Tobacco and Firearms, Jan. 22, 1996; data on high schools: Department of Education, Educational Demographics Unit, 1994; data on libraries: California State Library, Library Services Bureau, 1994; data on McDonald's: McDonald's Corporate Headquarters, 1996.

to life: McDonald's restaurants seem to be everywhere, but there are more than 10 times as many firearms dealers. At the same time, the comparison brings into the frame images related to young people—schools and libraries—so the audience is reminded of the things society could be providing more of for children and youth.

• **Provide ironic comparisons.** For example, a child care advocacy group noted that child care workers make less than $10 per hour whereas prison guards are paid more than $18 per hour. The ironic comparison helped call into question society's priorities and perhaps suggested the notion that good early childhood care can prevent criminal behavior later.

   Such comparisons can be made on both sides of an issue, of course. As a Cato Institute policy analysis on campaign spending noted, "To say that too much money is spent on campaigning is to beg the question, compared to what? . . . Americans spend more than twice as much money each year on yogurt as on political campaigns."[23]

• **Personalize the number.** For example, community residents near a gasoline refinery noted that the plant emits 6 tons of pollutants per day—or 25 balloons full of toxic pollution for each school child in the town.[24] The personalized statistic was much more vivid and immediate than the overall number of six tons per day.

ADVOCACY IN ACTION: Social Math on Child Care

Advocates for high quality, affordable child care used social math to reframe their issue as one of economic health. The economy of Santa Cruz County depends on agriculture, and the advocates were able to use this to make their point about how child care contributes to the community. The Santa Cruz County Office of Education Child Development Resource Center, in a project with the National Economic Development and Law Center, determined that child care, as a business, contributes $30 million a year to Santa Cruz County's economy—more than lettuce ($27.1 million) or raspberries ($27.1 million), and almost as much as roses and apples combined ($32 million). They held a news conference to present this information (see Figure 4.2), highlight concerns about the child care shortages in the county, and call on local industry to invest in child care.

Comparing the value of child care to lettuce and raspberries effectively made the case for child care as a social good, and the comparison was featured prominently in the news coverage. No one in Santa Cruz County has to be told about the value of those crops to the local economy, but few had probably ever considered the child care industry in the same light or suspected that it contributed as much as the cash crops. The group's use of social math effectively positioned child care as an important issue for everyone who lives in the county, whether or not they have children.

Figure 4.2 title: **Child Care is Good Business**

Figure 4.2. Child Care Advocates Use Social Math
SOURCE: Chart designed by the Santa Cruz County Office of Education, Marcia Meyer and Suzan Mark, 1997.

Identify authentic voices

One of the most effective things you can do to help frame stories from a policy perspective is to put journalists in touch with people who have had direct experience with the problem you are trying to solve. Reporters need to have a personal story to illustrate the topics they cover; it is a critical requirement of the news format. The challenge for advocates is to help personalize the story enough to make it compelling for the audience, but not so much that they will blame the victim.

Fortunately, many advocates are people who have directly experienced the problem and become active in efforts to address it. These "victims" have unique power to shape news coverage through their authentic stories. In fact, they have transformed themselves from victims to advocates.

If you know of such people who would like to talk with journalists, it is important to work with them in advance so they feel prepared and comfort-

---

Checklist: Framing

1. Translate individual problem to a social issue.
2. Assign primary responsibility.
3. Present a solution.
4. Make a practical appeal.
5. Develop story elements:
   - compelling visuals and symbols
   - media bites
   - social math
   - authentic voices

---

able. Also, they should be able to talk about the policy solution, just as any other advocate would. Advocates should be prepared to shift from their personal experience to the policy issue. For example, journalists will ask someone who has suffered a loss, "How do you feel about what happened?" This question should be the starting point for a statement that illuminates who shares responsibility for prevention, such as, "I feel angry that the city council has not done more to respect my right, and my family's right, to breathe clean air. They must pass the clean air ordinance now."

ADVOCACY IN ACTION: "My husband almost died . . ."

The most powerful advocates are often those who have had direct experience with the problem. In Livermore, California, a law enforcement officer was shot with a small handgun by a driver he had pulled over on a routine traffic stop. His wife became a strong advocate for banning these junk handguns in her town. When she told us her story for the first time, she cried as she described how her husband had nearly been killed; she then apologized for the emotion. We assured her, however, that not only were her feelings natural, they were a powerful part of her role in the advocacy effort she had joined. She replied, "It's good to know some good can come out of the pain."

Advocates should never hesitate to acknowledge their emotions in retelling their stories, *if they feel comfortable doing so.* It makes the story stronger for reporters and the message louder for policymakers. But they should also try not to be derailed by emotion; they must keep their focus on the policy approach they are advocating.

Summary

Our fifth rule is: Supply journalists with creative story elements that illustrate the solution you support. Because the way issues are framed helps news consumers decide who is responsible for the cause and solution of a problem, it is critical to pay attention to framing.

To frame your issue effectively, remember to:

- Know what you want to say before trying to attract media attention or talking to a journalist
- Anticipate different ways to shift from the inevitable questions that imply the problem is solely one of personal responsibility to answers that highlight the shared institutional accountability
- Prepare several illustrations to support your points, using compelling visuals, well-conceived media bites, social math, and other good story elements.

News coverage conveys credibility and legitimacy on an issue. By planning in advance to frame your issue from a progressive perspective, you can increase the likelihood not only that you will get the coverage, but that your issue will be covered in ways that increase support for the policies you promote.

Notes

1. Kosicki, G. (1993). Problems and opportunities in agenda-setting research. *Journal of Communication, 43*(2), 100-127.

2. There are many other, more complex meanings of the term *framing* used in the fields of linguistics and sociology; for our purposes in strategic media work, we use this practical definition.

3. Ryan, C. (1991). *Prime time activism.* Boston: South End Press.

4. Iyengar, S. (1991). *Is anyone responsible? How television frames political issues.* Chicago: University of Chicago Press.

5. Iyengar, 1991. An additional problem revealed in Iyengar's research is that when the person featured in the story is African American, viewers respond by blaming the victim even in stories that focus on the context rather than the individual. His analysis suggests that racial stereotypes run so deep that they are not overcome by contextual news frames.

6. Suro, R. (1993, January 11). Pollution-weary minorities try civil rights tack. *The New York Times,* p. A1.

7. Dorfman, L. (1994). *News operations: How television reports on health.* Doctoral dissertation, University of California at Berkeley.

8. *Beyond Affliction: The Disability History Project,* Straight Ahead Pictures, Inc., 1997. Tapes and transcripts of this 4-hour radio series broadcast on National Public Radio can be ordered by calling (303) 823-8000. Also see http://www.npr/org/programs/disability.

9. Hardin, P. (1996, March 28). Congress holds "smoking gun": Cigarette machines not out by deadline." *Richmond Times-Dispatch,* p. A1.

10. Shaw, R. (1996). *The activist's handbook: A primer for the 1990s and beyond.* Berkeley: University of California Press.

11. Television interview, Sacramento, June 10, 1998.

12. Hilts, P. (1995, March 9). Head of FDA calls smoking pediatric disease. *The New York Times*, p. A11.

13. Hayden, T. (1997, February 10). Be equally tough on causes of violence. *Los Angeles Times*, p. B5.

14. Sample, H. (1997, January 10). Boxer proposes ban on sale of "junk guns." *Sacramento Bee*, p. A3.

15. Quoted in the Advocacy Institute's *Trumpet Notes*, *1*(3), page 5, February 1996.

16. Testimony at Sacramento City Council meeting, May 14, 1996.

17. Rauch, Kate Darby. (1997, May 29). UC students' design may curtail GG suicide jumps. *West County Times*, p. A4.

18. Local Chicago TV news coverage, May 31, 1991.

19. For an in-depth primer on social math, see By the numbers: A guide to the tactical use of statistics for positive policy change. *Blowing Smoke Advisory* No. 2. Washington, DC: The Advocacy Institute.

20. Eng, T., & Butler, W. (Eds.). (1997). *The hidden epidemic: Confronting sexually transmitted diseases.* Washington, DC: Committee on Prevention and Control of Sexually Transmitted Diseases, Institute of Medicine, National Academy of Sciences.

21. Incidence of initiation of cigarette smoking—United States, 1965-1996. (1998, October 9). *Morbidity and Mortality Weekly Report* (MMWR), *47*(39).

22. Toner, R. (1993, May 4). In health-care debate, Canada plan still lives. *New York Times*, p. A22.

23. Smith, B. (1995, September 13). *Campaign finance regulation: Faulty assumptions and undemocratic consequences*, Cato Institute document cited in Engle, M. (1996, March/April). Yogurt, antacid, and politics: The selling of the underselling of America. Extra!, p. 10.

24. Cummings, P., Jacobs, J., & Stevenson, M. A. (1994). *Chevron reformulated fuels project media plan.* Unpublished manuscript, prepared for the Richmond Neighborhood Health Center, Richmond, CA.

5

CREATING NEWS

If you don't like the news, go out and make some of your own.

News analyst Scoop Nisker

News happens, but not always spontaneously. News is also created. Once you have identified which elements of newsworthiness are present in your story and have thought about how to provide a journalist with a story that will reinforce your policy goals, you can begin to strategize about what type of news presence would best accomplish your goals and how you might get that access. For instance, when an issue has not been on the public or media agenda, or when you want to mobilize the local community and make your demands urgent for policymakers, a colorful, live press event such as a rally or demonstration might be appropriate. When you have specific arguments you want to advance on an issue that is already being covered, an op-ed piece may best serve your goals. The main options for calling attention to your story are to create news or to piggyback on breaking news. As we will discuss in Chapters 7 and 8, you can also use the editorial pages, create paid advertisements, or adopt other strategies.

Creating news means doing something that is worth telling a story about. It can be as simple as issuing a report, presenting a demand, or making a public announcement. News releases, news conferences, and demonstrations are common vehicles for creating news. In brainstorming how to create news, be

Create News

sure to pay attention to the tenets of newsworthiness described in Chapter 3. Your objective is to do something so interesting, groundbreaking, or compelling that journalists will virtually *have* to cover your story.

This can take some creativity, but there are many interesting newsworthy stories about every issue advocates work on. For instance, if you are concerned about cuts in food stamp funding, you could issue a report that would describe and quantify the precise effects of those cuts on the typical family. For an even more compelling story, however, challenge your elected officials to live for a week on a food-stamp budget. Invite reporters to come grocery shopping with you to see what the new funding levels will buy an average family. Ask people who receive food stamps to talk to reporters about the difficult choices they have to make and how the funding cuts will further limit their nutritional options. Any one of these would make a compelling news story that would help enhance the impact of your report.

ADVOCACY IN ACTION: Creating News on the Budweiser Frogs

The Center on Alcohol Advertising was concerned about the impact of beer ads on young people. To put the issue on the media agenda, they conducted a survey of 221 fourth- and fifth-graders, asking them to identify the slogans uttered by such memorable cartoon characters as Bugs Bunny, Tony the Tiger, Smokey Bear, and the Budweiser Frogs. The results showed kids were as familiar with the Frogs' slogan "Bud-Wei-Ser" as with Tony the Tiger's "They're grrrreat!" or Bugs' "What's up, Doc?" In fact, among young boys in particular, the Budweiser Frogs' slogan was the best known, making the point that kids pay attention to, remember, and are influenced by beer ads featuring cartoon-like characters. The report generated coverage in *USA Today*[1] (see Figure 5.1) and many local papers around the country. It allowed the Center on Alcohol Advertising to put the issue of beer ads and kids on the public agenda.

Piggyback on Breaking News

Often, news stories last only one day. You can expand news attention by linking a breaking news story to your issue, an effective way to attract news coverage or get a letter to the editor or op-ed piece printed. The term *breaking news* refers to the hottest, most recent stories, those that are unfolding as they are being reported. A breaking news story can raise the salience of an issue for media gatekeepers. For example, if in May 1994 you pitched a story about a new counseling program for men who batter their partners, you might have been met with limited interest on reporters' part. However, if you pitched the same story just a month later, after the murders of Nicole Brown Simpson and Ron Goldman brought O. J. Simpson's history of domestic violence to light, your story would likely have gotten a much better reception.

It is often possible to piggyback on national stories by emphasizing the importance of the topic for local residents. National stories about welfare reform present opportunities for pitching local stories on successful programs or the potential consequences of changes in federal policy. For example, one

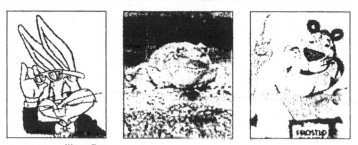

Warner Bros.

Eh, what's up Bud? Critics say it's not so terrific that kids rank Budweiser's frogs alongside Bugs Bunny and Tony the Tiger.

Critics say Bud ads too ribbet-ing for kids

By Bruce Horovitz
USA TODAY

Budweiser's talking frogs may be croaking to the wrong audience: kids.

Elementary school kids are more familiar with Budweiser's cartoon frogs crooning "Bud-wei-ser" than they are with Tony the Tiger roaring "They're grrreat!" about Kellogg's Frosted Flakes.

Even Smokey Bear's warning — "Only you can prevent forest fires" — is less memorable to kids 9 to 11 years old than the Bud frog ads, says a survey by the Center on Alcohol Advertising, a California-based consumer group.

The results of the survey of 221 fourth- and fifth-graders from seven San Francisco Bay-area schools were unveiled Wednesday just before the annual shareholders meeting of beer giant Anheuser-Busch, maker of Budweiser.

The group asked the brewer to stop airing ads that appeal to kids. "After a single year of advertising, the Budweiser frogs have assumed a friendly place in our children's psyches between Bugs Bunny and Smokey Bear," said Laurie Leiber, who conducted the study.

While 73% of the kids knew what the frogs say, a slightly larger number — 80% — knew that Bugs Bunny says, "Eh, what's up Doc?"

But Anheuser-Busch officials say they don't target kids. And they won't yank the frogs.

"Watching a beer ad does not cause a kid to drink," says Francine Katz, Anheuser's head of consumer awareness.

Consumer groups have become increasingly critical of beer and tobacco advertisers they believe target kids.

Anheuser has faced similar criticism for using figures, such as former spokesdog Spuds MacKenzie, that appeal to kids.

Figure 5.1. A Survey With a Message
SOURCE: Copyright 1996, *USA Today*. Reprinted with permission.

of the main problems of moving people from welfare to work is the lack of available public transportation. This provides an opportunity for local advocates to pitch stories about the need to expand public transportation from the cities to where the jobs are.

When you are confronted with a breaking news story that links to your issue, you need to act quickly to take advantage of the opportunity it presents. An effective and relatively easy approach is to write a letter to the editor

An effective and relatively easy approach is to write a letter to the editor pointing out the connection between the breaking story and your issue. For example, if you see a story on state spending on medical care related to tobacco use, you could write a letter saying that it would be more cost-effective in the long run to spend money on prevention approaches that reduce tobacco consumption in the first place. For practice linking your story to breaking news, see *Try It Out* at the end of this chapter.

ADVOCACY IN ACTION: Piggybacking on Breaking News

In the summer of 1998, the impotence drug Viagra was a hot news story across the country. A group concerned about many insurance companies' failure to cover birth control drugs for women took advantage of the buzz over Viagra to get their issue on the media agenda. They called reporters' attention to the irony and injustice inherent in insurance policies that paid for Viagra for men while denying women help in avoiding unwanted pregnancies. Their efforts paid off with a front-page story in *The New York Times*[2] (see Figure 5.2) and renewed focus on possible legislative measures to remedy the discrepancy.

Using Anniversaries to Create News

News stories are often linked to prior news events. For example, every November 22, there will be news stories relating back to President Kennedy's assassination, and every April 4, stories relating to Martin Luther King, Jr.'s assassination. Local anniversaries can also provide news hooks. Each April, you can expect to see stories that report on how Oklahoma City has recovered since the 1995 bombing of the Federal building and related stories on security, militia groups, and the like.

You can anticipate anniversaries to make stories about your issue more newsworthy. In Figure 5.3, we provide as an example a year's worth of anniversaries that might be used to call attention to issues related to gun injury and death; at the end of the chapter, we provide a worksheet to help you generate your own year of opportunities to make news on your issue. (See *Try It Out* at the end of this chapter.) The idea is not to suggest you should create news for each of these dates but rather to illustrate the possibilities of creating news any time of the year.

Background Questions for Planning Media Events

Although creating news can be a useful tactic, be sure that you are using your resources wisely. Too often, people rush to put on a formal media event, such as a news conference or demonstration, without thinking through whether the event is the best thing they could do to meet their strategic goals. These events take a great deal of time and energy to organize; if you're going to invest those resources, first, make sure that the event will be the right thing to do. You may be able to get the same effect by simply talking on the phone to reporters

PRESSURE GROWING TO COVER THE COST OF BIRTH CONTROL

LAWMAKERS ARE LOBBIED

Supporters See Unfairness in Plans That Cover Viagra but Not Family Planning

By PETER T. KILBORN

WASHINGTON, Aug. 1 — Seizing upon the celebrity of the male impotency pill Viagra, family planning groups are pressing lawmakers in Congress and the states on a long-ignored demand that employers cover the costs of contraception as a health benefit. They are confronting lawmakers with the inequity they see in some employers' covering Viagra while denying women help in avoiding unwanted pregnancies.

Gloria Feldt, president of the Planned Parenthood Foundation of America, which has been leading the lobbying in Congress for birth control coverage, said, "The groundswell is there."

Maryland was the first state to mandate coverage of prescription contraceptives in workers' health insurance plans, approving a bill in April. At least a dozen other states are weighing similar measures.

In Congress, the Senate and House have approved provisions, attached to appropriations bills, that would require the Federal Government to offer all commonly prescribed forms of contraception, including birth control pills, intrauterine devices and diaphragms, to its 2.4 million employees who have health insurance.

Figure 5.2. Family Planning Groups Use Viagra to Make News
SOURCE: Copyright 1998 by *The New York Times*. Reprinted with permission.

following your issue, or pitching an "exclusive" story to one interested reporter at a prominent news organization, rather than trying to attract many journalists to an event.

Rule 6:
Make your news events count.

When deciding what kind of news event will work best for your story, or whether to have a formal event at all, consider the following strategic questions:

Why do you want to have this event?

You should have a specific objective every time you seek media coverage. Examples include: to call attention to an issue, to call for action on the part of a government official or other target, to make the public aware of an upcoming policy-related event, or to establish your organization as a credible source of information and leadership on an issue.

Is a news event the best way to reach those goals?

It takes time and energy for reporters to come out to an event; try to save such events for occasions that will really be worth journalists' energy, and yours. Consider whether you can be more effective with a mailing and follow-up phone calls to selected journalists or an editorial board visit.

What is the objective of this specific event?

Focusing on a single clear objective lets you make the most of the media opportunity.

If you're certain that a news conference, demonstration, or other media event is appropriate, your next step is to focus on the outcome you want from the event. Decide what message you want reporters to walk away with. Incorporate two or three focused statements into all your materials. For example, if your event highlights a variety of successful violence-prevention programs, your recurring statement may be, "Violence prevention programs work; our state legislature should fund more of them." Focusing on a single clear objective lets you make the most of the media opportunity.

Why should the media be interested in covering your event?

Reporters have to tell good stories, and you will be more likely to get news coverage if you can plan in advance to provide them with newsworthy elements. Highlight the parts of your story or event that are unusual, interesting, controversial, or otherwise compelling for journalists and their audiences, as described in Chapter 3.

Having a successful media event depends on systematic planning as well as on the news value of your story. There are many decisions to be made and contingencies to be planned for before, during, and after the event.

Planning Media Events

Before the event

- **Decide on the best time for your event.** Hold events at times when you are more likely to get media coverage. On weekday mornings, the best time is generally 10 a.m. News conferences held after 2 p.m. are less likely to be well attended. Saturdays tend to be slower for news organizations, so the benefit of holding your event then is that you compete with fewer events elsewhere; of course, the trade-off is that fewer people read and watch the news on weekends. You may be able to link the timing of your event to an anniversary or holiday that increases the newsworthiness of your story. For instance, holding a rally for funding of programs involving Native Americans on Columbus Day or around Thanksgiving may give you more of a hook for news coverage than at other times of the year, because of the connection between Indian history and the events commemorated by these holidays.

- **Start media outreach early.** Identify the journalists you want to contact, and make sure you have accurate names, addresses, and fax numbers for them. Mail or fax a media advisory or news release at least three days before the event and, if you can, again around 6 a.m. the morning of the event. (See pages 83-84 and *Try It Out* at the end of this chapter for how-to's on writing news advisories and releases.) A typical TV newsroom in a major U.S. city gets hundreds of news releases by fax each day, so be sure to use big bold print to makes yours stand out, and follow up with a phone call.

- **Follow up with journalists.** A day or two before the event, follow up your faxed or mailed news release with a phone call making sure it was received and offering to answer any questions before the event.

- **Try to time your pitch well.** It's important to give the right amount of advance notice for media events—too much time in advance is almost as bad as too little. Most journalists and editors at daily news outlets plan no more than a few days in advance, and unless they are doing an in-depth print story, they probably won't work on something coming up in three weeks. Send your media advisory up to a week in advance, but don't call until the event is closer. In most cases, your first pitch, accompanied by a complete news release, should be two to three days before the event, with follow-up calls the day before.

- **Try to avoid conflicting with other events.** Some conflicts can be avoided if you know what else will be happening that day. For example, don't plan a news conference too close to a major election or during other predict-

Example: Dates to Make News on Guns

Certain anniversaries provide an opportunity for news coverage of gun-related issues. Some might be events that reporters will cover routinely, and advocates can provide a new angle on the story; others might not be covered unless advocates provide the impetus. You can anticipate these dates (or similar anniversaries related to your own issue) and be ready with a news event, letter, or op-ed piece linking the anniversary to your policy solution. For instance, a gun control advocate could start a letter with the observation, "In the year since the Littleton, Colorado, schoolyard shooting, [how many] other children have been the victims of gun violence."

Here are some dates that provide hooks for coverage of sensible gun policies:

January

16	Ennis Cosby, Bill Cosby's son, shot to death in Los Angeles (1997)
17	Stockton, California, schoolyard assault gun shooting (1989)
20	Martin Luther King, Jr.'s birthday (a federal holiday)

February

President's Day	Presidents shot or shot at: Lincoln, Garfield, McKinley, Theodore Roosevelt, Franklin Roosevelt, Truman, Kennedy, Ford, Reagan
28	Anniversary of the Brady Law, requiring a waiting period and background check for gun purchases, going into effect (1994)

March

31	Latina musician Selena shot to death (1995)

April

1	Musician Marvin Gaye shot and killed (1984)
4	Martin Luther King, Jr.'s assassination (1967)
20	Littleton, Colorado: Two boys, ages 17 and 18, killed 12 classmates and a teacher before killing themselves at Columbine High School. Many others were injured. (1999)

May

Mother's Day	Many parents who have lost children to gun violence get media attention on Mother's Day

June

5	Robert F. Kennedy's assassination (1968)

July

1	Shootings at law offices at 101 California Street, San Francisco, kill nine and wound six (1993)
4	"Independence" from fear of violence

August

1	Charles Whitman opens fire from the University of Texas Tower in Austin, shooting 46 people (1966)

September

7	Rap musician Tupac Shakur shot (1996)
13	Tupac Shakur died (1996)

October

22	Federal legislation to ban the import of Saturday night specials signed and went into effect (1968)

November

22	John F. Kennedy's assassination (1963)

December

1	Paducah, Kentucky, a 14-year-old boy shot and killed three high school girls and wounded five others (1997)
8	Former Beatle John Lennon shot and killed (1980)

Other anniversary/milestone dates to link gun news to could be local, for example, the anniversary of your city's date for voting to ban junk guns. The annual release of crime statistics by the federal government (National Crime Victimization Survey, Uniform Crime Reports), as well as state and county agencies, offers another opportunity. You might want to tally the number of gun deaths since legislature convened, since the beginning of the decade, or since the import ban in 1968 on Saturday night specials; another day is to find the last day your city or state went without a gun death.

Figure 5.3

ably busy news times. Of course, "acts of God" can preempt your story despite your best efforts.

• **Choose and train your spokespeople early.** Identify one goal or mission that you want the public (via the media) to know from your media event. The spokesperson or people should be prepared to give this message in a media bite (a short, concise, fresh message about your goal). Spokespeople should be informed and knowledgeable about the issue. Conduct speakers' training prior to the event. Try to have an "authentic voice"—someone with personal experience with the issue—to tell his or her personal story and to advocate for the policy. Reporters need someone to profile and will be more likely to cover your story if you provide them with such a person.

• **Be sure to emphasize the newsworthiness of your event.** Highlight the angle that lets journalists know why your story is *interesting* and *important*. The newsworthy angle(s) of the story should be emphasized in all your materials as well as in your pitch, which should be timed to take advantage of any news hooks. For example, stories on ballot initiatives will become increasingly newsworthy as an election approaches.

At the event

• **Simplify the issue.** Advocacy issues are often complicated, whereas a journalist's mandate is to tell simple stories. Try to simplify your issue as much as possible. Present the story to reporters the way they would present it to the public—you will improve your chances of good coverage. Identify two or

Checklist: Media Event Planning Time Line

One month in advance

Decide on objective and key messages of the event.
Decide on a newsworthy "hook" for the event.
Find a site for the event.
Brainstorm some interesting visual elements that will reinforce the key messages of the event: charts, ads, demonstrators with signs, and so on.
Arrange for speakers.
Update media list, if necessary.
Begin planning media kit materials (see Checklist: The Media Kit).

Two weeks in advance

Draft media advisory and news release.
Draft fact sheets, speakers' bios, and other media kit materials.
Assign roles for people at the event (media greeter, emcee, speakers, etc.).
With speakers, draft talking points.

One week to three days before

Fax media advisory (including directions to event site) and news release.
Follow up by calling journalists to pitch the story to them.
Compile media kits.
Conduct speakers' training.
Create sign-in sheet for attending journalists.
Create table tents, name tags, or other means of identifying speakers.

The day before

Make follow-up calls; re-fax the advisory and news release to key media contacts.
Make sure media kits and all other conference materials are ready.
Deliver media kits to any journalists who requested materials in advance.
Make sure journalists have directions to the site.
Rehearse the event with speakers, if possible. Ask every question that could possibly be important, and prepare for every possible problem.

At the event

Introduce each speaker; keep comments to three minutes maximum.
Leave time for questions after all speakers have presented.
After the formal presentation, help reporters connect with individual speakers for one-on-one interviews.
For more, see Checklist: At the News Conference, page 81.

After the event

Send media kits to any journalists who didn't attend.
Call journalists who attended, offering to answer further questions.
Track and evaluate coverage to see how you can improve next time.

Checklist: At the News Conference

- **Is your room large enough to hold the invited number of journalists, plus a few more?** *Always leave yourself plenty of room for last-minute attendees.*

- **Is there parking nearby for attendees?** *If necessary, have signs directing attendees from the parking lot to the conference site.*

- **Can the conference site accommodate TV cameras?** *Are there enough (and powerful enough) electrical outlets and extension cords for cameras and lights?*

- **Make sure your office is staffed before, during, and after the conference.** *That way, the media can reach someone to get directions or additional information if necessary.*

- **Set up a check-in table near the entrance where you can greet arriving journalists.** *Make sure you have extra media kits and other background materials.*

- **Have a complete list of invited media and check them off as they arrive, or create a sign-in sheet for names, addresses, and affiliations of all attendees.** *Keep track of every media representative there, and use the information to update your files later.*

- **Give each attendee a press kit, including an agenda for the conference.** *Have spare pens and paper available.*

- **Have an emcee introduce all speakers.** *Make your speakers and guests available for post-conference interviews, in person and by phone.*

- **Are presentation materials prepared?** *Make sure the slides are right side up; pretest the overhead projector or slide projector and have a spare bulb available. Have two copies of any video or audiotapes you are going to play in case one of them breaks.*

- **Will you need amplification for your speakers?** *If so, check in advance to be sure your microphones work and are set to appropriate sound levels.*

- **Are there refreshments available?** *Providing coffee, donuts, and the like for reporters is a nice touch, although not essential. At a minimum, be sure speakers have water available.*

---

three concise, salient points that you can state clearly and often. But heed Albert Einstein's advice: "Make things as simple as possible, but not one bit simpler." There is a fine line between simplification and trivialization.

- **Hold your media event at an accessible area.** Hold events at central locations, as close to the news outlets you've targeted as possible. Let journalists know in advance about parking availability. If the event is outside, avoid noisy or windy areas. If indoors, be sure there are electrical hookups available for photographers' lights.

- **Help reporters identify the right people to interview.** At the event, be sure to introduce spokespeople to reporters, and have them available for interviews.

- **Provide interesting visuals.** Especially for TV, compelling visual images are mandatory for getting coverage. Part of your pitch should be to let journalists know what visual opportunities will be accessible to them at your event. Describe visuals to them when you call or write.

- **Provide a media kit with fact sheets and other materials that are accurate and complete.** The point of the media kit is to gather key information on your event in one place and make journalists' jobs as easy as possible. If a reporter is on a tight deadline, he or she may not have time to track down all the supporting data, and may have to shelve a piece if there's not enough substance. To avoid this, provide accurate fact sheets with full reference listings. After the event, reporters will consult the materials you distributed. News releases and media packets should include a clearly designated contact person and phone number for further information. Make sure the contact person will be available at that phone number immediately after the event and during the time that the news is "hot." When possible, offer a home phone or cell phone number.

After the event

- **Follow up with journalists.** You should contact all reporters who attended the event to see if they need any further information. (To know who attended, be sure to have a media sign-in area at the event.) Most journalists will tell you if they are planning to do a piece on your story. Send media kits to journalists who didn't attend the event, and call them to see if they would like more information or an interview.

- **Evaluate what went wrong if you don't get the coverage you'd hoped.** If the coverage doesn't turn out as you'd hoped, it is not always your fault. If an earthquake hits the morning of your event, or all the journalists you contacted get reassigned by their editors, you're out of luck. If you find out early enough that something big is going to preempt your story, it may be worth postponing your event. Otherwise, just hope for better luck next time. The time you spent may still have been productive, even if there was little or no coverage. The fact sheets and other background materials you provided will help to educate journalists, and the relationships you strengthened can help advance your issue in the future, even though your story didn't get covered this time. On the other hand, if you think your issue or event wasn't newsworthy enough, or you picked a bad day or time for the event, apply what you've learned to your future media efforts.

Checklist: The Media Kit

A media kit can be as simple as a news release stapled to a fact sheet or as detailed as many sheets of information in glossy folders. You could include:

- The most recent news release, including contacts' names and phone and fax numbers. (Don't assume the reporters will have a copy of the news release, despite your multiple faxes.)
- Fact sheets including official sources for all facts and figures. (Of course, make sure they are accurate.)
- List of speakers with affiliations, brief bios, and contact phone numbers.
- Informational fliers or brochures.
- Copies of articles that have been written about your issue or op-ed pieces you have had published. These will add credibility and help the reporters, editors, and producers produce a well-informed story.
- Background information on the organization, including phone and fax numbers.

ADVOCACY IN ACTION: Youth Speak Out Against Violence

In Oakland, California, a group called Teens-On-Target has successfully used media events to call attention to the violence in their community while pressuring community leaders to enact legislation to ban junk guns. For one media event, called in response to three youth shootings in one week, the youth chose a cemetery as the backdrop, to reinforce the tragedy of children killed by guns. In preparation for the conference, the youth practiced over and over their comments on how to stop gun violence; limiting guns to sporting use only and getting local police to crack down on illegal gun dealers were two of the solutions they focused on. Although one TV reporter said that the site was too far away for her to come, *The Oakland Tribune* sent a reporter and covered the event. This success spurred the group to further advocacy efforts: To date, the youth of Teens-On-Target have attended and testified at 90% of all city council hearings where gun legislation was considered.

How to Write a Media Advisory

A media advisory is like an invitation to your media event. It contains only the key information journalists need to know to decide whether to cover the event and where and when it will take place. Fax or mail the media advisory any time from 3 weeks to 24 hours before the event. Follow up with a phone call and/or a more detailed news release within a couple days of the event.

Format your media advisory as shown at the end of this chapter, using your organization's letterhead. At the bottom of the page, the symbols # # # or -30- signal the end of the advisory. (See *Try It Out* at the end of this chapter.)

How to Write a   The news release is more in-depth than an advisory. It is written like a news
News Release   story, including an attention-grabbing headline, sharp lead paragraph, background facts, quotes, and details on the policy issue you are advocating. Think
of this as your opportunity to write the ideal news story on your issue. Many
wire services and radio news departments rely heavily on the verbatim text of
news releases for their stories; other news departments will write their own
stories from scratch but may use some of the facts and quotes in your news
release.

       Format the release as shown at the end of this chapter, on your letterhead.
Each paragraph should be no longer than four to five lines, with text double-
spaced. Try to keep the whole release to two pages at most. Don't split
paragraphs between pages. (See *Try It Out* at the end of this chapter.)

       A couple of days before the event, fax your news release to every journalist
you are inviting. Make follow-up calls the day before the event to remind
reporters. Include a copy of the release in the media kits to be distributed at
the event as well.

ADVOCACY IN ACTION: Resources for Youth Press Conference

As part of The California Wellness Foundation's Violence Prevention Initiative (VPI), advocates across the state
worked to support violence prevention programs that could make a difference for youth in their local communities:
full-service schools, mentoring and tutoring programs, job training, and recreation opportunities. When state
policy leaders were in budget negotiations over how to spend the 1998 budget surplus of $4 billion, the VPI
members wanted to communicate to legislators the need to fund these crucial resources for youth. Martin &
Glantz, a firm dedicated to grassroots organizing and public education, organized a media event at the state capitol
that had three critical components:

- Republican and Democratic pollsters presented public opinion research showing that voters supported
and were willing to pay for such programs. The release of these polling data was the news hook for the conference.
- Youth from across the state spoke about what such resources meant to them and how they made a difference.
The young people provided an authentic perspective and a way for reporters to personalize the story.
- Representatives from law enforcement, public health, and the PTA also called on lawmakers to help
neighborhoods help themselves to prevent violence. They demonstrated that this coalition should be taken
seriously because its members had significant collective clout.

Behind the speakers at the news conference, large, colorful maps of each community showed where the young
people had identified schools, parks, and other local resources that could be strengthened to help reduce violence.
Speakers worked in advance to be clear about their talking points. And on the day of the media event, Martin &
Glantz placed a paid ad in the *Sacramento Bee,* describing how public opinion supported violence prevention
programs and calling on lawmakers to invest in these programs. Together, these elements made the Resources
for Youth news conference a powerful story that generated coverage across the state.

Our sixth rule is: **Make your news events count.** Creating news means having something that is worth telling a story about. This can mean issuing a new report, holding a demonstration, or putting forth a new solution to an old problem. Sometimes you can "piggyback" on breaking news by linking your issue to another story that is getting covered in the news. Anniversaries are a good way to create news because news organizations can be counted on to revisit major issues at regular intervals, especially if you provide them with the elements of a good story and make it easy for them to cover it.

This chapter has focused on the logistics of planning and carrying out good news events. But the most critical element of any news event is being well prepared to talk to journalists. When reporters call or show up, you must know what to tell them; this is the topic of the next chapter.

Summary

Notes

1. Horovitz, B. (1996, April 25). Critics say Bud ads too ribbet-ing for kids. *USA Today,* p. 1B.

2. Kilborn, P. (1998, August). Pressure growing to cover the cost of birth control. *New York Times,* p. 1A.

TRY IT OUT: Piggybacking Exercise

To try out piggy-backing yourself, pick up a copy of your local newspaper. Carefully look through each section; your objective is to find a news item or opinion piece that relates to your issue, whether directly or indirectly. For instance:

- Can you provide facts or a perspective that would localize a national story? Reporters are often interested in making national news relevant to their local audience. A local flood may highlight the importance of the national Federal Emergency Management Agency program and help underscore the need for full funding of such assistance programs.

- Can you expand the perspective to build on one of the local stories? You may spot an interesting story that you think doesn't go far enough. If the news reports on construction of a new manufacturing plant, that may be an opportunity for you and your group to raise the issue of environmental impact, labor issues, or other related concerns.

Now present the article to the rest of your group members by answering the following questions:

Why does this news article or opinion piece provide an opportunity to gain media coverage for your issue? _____

_____

How would you describe this connection in, say, a letter to the editor? _____

_____

TRY IT OUT: LOCAL ANNIVERSARY WORKSHEET

Answer the questions below to identify potential local news hooks for creating news. There may be some events you can think of that have a direct link to your issue, like a yearly candlelight march for peace. There also might be community events that don't have an obvious connection. For example, Juneteenth, September 16, and July 4 are all times for celebrating freedom. Violence prevention advocates have used these events, which the whole community participates in, to call for "freedom from fear of guns." Be creative—list all the important local events you can, then see how they might link to your issue.

What event happens every year in my community that the whole neighborhood participates in or is aware of? _____

_____

What regional, state, or national events does this community or neighborhood pay attention to every year? _____

_____

What links are there between our issue and any of the events listed above? _____

_____

TRY IT OUT: WRITING A MEDIA ADVISORY

Here are some guidelines for preparing a media advisory. It includes all the necessary elements and a brief description of the information you should provide. A sample is shown in Figure 5.4.

FOR IMMEDIATE RELEASE   CONTACT: (Name)
(Today's date)   (Phone Number)

MEDIA ADVISORY HEADLINE: KEEP IT SHORT, ALL CAPITAL LETTERS

WHAT: _____ (two to three sentences on what is happening)
WHEN: _____ (Date and time)
WHERE:_____ (Address)
WHO:_____ (Names of people or organizations involved)
WHY: _____ (two or three sentences that highlight why this event is
                         important and newsworthy)

# # #

STOP GUN VIOLENCE
THE CALIFORNIA STREET MARCH

WHO: The California Street March Committee, a group of citizens, including friends and family of the victims of the 101 California Street massacre that occurred on July 1, 1993.

WHAT: To mark the one year anniversary of the massacre, the Committee has organized a commemorative march to be followed by a program honoring the eight people who died and the six who were wounded in the massacre. Failed businessman Gian Luigi Ferri killed and wounded the victims in the highrise office building with two semi-automatic assault weapons. He then took his own life.

In addition, the March will commemorate the 38,000 Americans who died of gunshot wounds in the United States during the last year. City officials, including the Mayor, support the March, and many church, civic, business and community organizations are expected to participate. Three hundred children, carrying "The Banner of Hope" will also take part. The Banner is a half-mile long panel inscribed with the names of over 8,000 children who were murdered in California in the last 10 years. All residents of the Bay Area are encouraged to join the March.

WHEN: The March will begin at 12 noon on Thursday, June 30th, 1994. The commemorative program will take place at the Embarcadero, beginning at 1 p.m.

WHERE: **Marchers will assemble at Grace Cathedral,** march down California Street past 101 California, and continue down Market Street to the Embarcadero.

WHY: The purpose of the California Street March is to remind the citizens of San Francisco and the United States of the tragedy of the massacre at 101 California Street, and to send a message to lawmakers protesting the rising tide of violence involving firearms.

"We seek a true memorial to our loved ones in laws that will protect the American people from having this kind of tragedy happen again."

Dr. Megin Scully, Committee Chair

101 California Street, Suite 1075, San Francisco, CA 94111
415-487-8709

Figure 5.4. Media Advisory: An Example

TRY IT OUT: WRITING A NEWS RELEASE

Here is a format for writing news releases. It includes all the necessary elements and what information you should provide in each place. A sample is shown in Figure 5.5.

FOR IMMEDIATE RELEASE   **CONTACT: (Name)**
(Today's date)   (Phone Number)

HEADLINE: KEEP IT SHORT, ALL CAPITAL LETTERS

1st Paragraph: What is happening, who is involved, where and when (briefly)

2nd Paragraph: Why this event is significant and newsworthy

3rd Paragraph: Quote from an expert involved that emphasizes how significant this
                             event is

4th Paragraph: More details on where and when the event is happening

5th+ Paragraphs: Other pertinent details, including:
                                 Speakers' names and affiliations
                                 Description of any photo opportunities
                                 Further quotes from other spokespeople

Final Paragraph: One-sentence "boiler plate" description of the organization(s) involved
                             in the event.

MORE (if release goes to a second page, or:)

(to indicate end)

FOR IMMEDIATE RELEASE

CONTACT: Leo McElroy -McElroy Communications
916-447-7415

Evelyn Aleman – Valencia, Perez & Echeveste
626-793-9335

454 Las Gallinas Avenue, Suite 178
San Rafael, California 94903-3618
T: 415 331-5991
F: 415 331-2969

Assembly Speaker Antonio Villaraigosa and A Unique Alliance of Youth and Statewide Leaders Will Discuss Strategies for Reducing Youth Violence and Present Findings of Local Mapping Projects

News Conference to Include an Analysis of Bipartisan Polling Results and Implications for State Budget Surplus

SACRAMENTO, Calif. – With polling results and maps in hand, California youth will join Assembly Speaker Antonio Villaraigosa, the president of the California State PTA and other statewide leaders to discuss strategies to reduce violence and present findings of local mapping projects at a Capitol news conference today.

The briefing, scheduled for 9:30 a.m. in the Speaker's Press Room, will also include bipartisan analysis of recent California polls by Democratic pollster Paul Maslin of Fairbank, Maslin, Maullin & Associates and Republican Pollster Ed Goeas of The Tarrance Group. Results of regional polls conducted in each of California's media markets indicate that voters prefer investment in prevention over incarceration as a strategy to reduce youth violence.

"Too many of our young people are victims of violence," said Villaraigosa. "It's clear that we in Sacramento must do more to effectively address this situation. We know there are many successful programs out there and we have to do our part to support them."

As the leading killer of youth in California, violence is a public health epidemic requiring a public response. News conference participants hope to convince legislative leaders that the wishes of California youth and voters need to be addressed in this year's budget negotiations.

"The views of Californians are clear," said pollster Paul Maslin. "Voters are looking for long-term solutions to the problem of violence in California and are ready and willing to invest tax dollars in prevention strategies to ensure the future of California's young people."

Figure 5.5a.   News Release: An Example

Youth/2-2-2

California youth agree. Using large maps provided by Thomas Bros. Maps® Educational Foundation, young people will present the results of mapping projects undertaken in their communities to identify potential to reduce violence against youth. These local efforts show what can be done in each of our neighborhoods to begin reducing youth violence. The strategies these communities have targeted – teen centers, safe parks, job training and keeping schools open – are just a few of the ways to help reduce violence against youth.

"The youth and the voters in our state are calling on Governor Wilson and the legislative leadership to invest public funds in effective violence prevention strategies," said Rosaline Turnball, president of the California State PTA. "Investments to keep schools open until 6:00 p.m. and to expand after-school activities are perfect examples of local programs our leaders should support."

Youth from Sacramento, San Francisco, Fresno, Inglewood, Pomona, Riverside and Escondido will be on hand to share the results of their local projects. Joining them will be

- Antonio Villaraigosa, Speaker of the California State Assembly;
- Gary L. Yates, president and CEO of The California Wellness Foundation and Frank Acosta, senior program officer for the Foundation;
- Pollsters Paul Maslin and Ed Goeas;
- Representatives from the Resources for Youth statewide partner organizations: California State PTA, California Police Chiefs Association, California Medical Association, Chief Probation Officers of California, and the League of Women Voters of California; and
- Beth Cantrell, executive director of Thomas Bros. Maps® Educational Foundation.

Resources for Youth is a public education campaign funded by a grant to Martin & Glantz LLC from The California Wellness Foundation.

Figure 5.5b. News Release: An Example

6

TALKING TO JOURNALISTS

---◆---

The relationship between sources and journalists resembles a dance, for sources seek access to journalists, and journalists seek access to sources. Although it takes two to tango, either journalists or sources can lead, but more often than not, sources do the leading.

Media researcher Herbert Gans

---◆---

Each time you talk to a journalist, you have the opportunity to educate him or her about your perspective. Advocates often forget that talking to journalists is a critical *strategic* activity. An interview is not a conversation, nor is it your chance for personal recognition; it is an opportunity for you to convey your key messages.

You will typically have one of three different types of interactions with journalists:

Proactive: when you call journalists to pitch a story about an issue or event. These are the easiest interactions to prepare for, because you are initiating the contact and suggesting the story.

Reactive: when you respond to a reporter's query. This chapter will help you be ready to respond to reporters' calls.

Self-defense: when you are asked to respond to a crisis or to "bad press." It is not the ideal situation but nevertheless presents an opportunity to advance your goals.

Each of these interactions with journalists requires focused attention to your overall advocacy goals. Your statements, whether proactive, reactive, or defensive, should further the message to your target.

When You Call a Journalist. . . .

Many advocates' first contact with a journalist comes when they call to "pitch" their story to a reporter, producer, or assignment desk editor. A pitch is a short description of your story and a concise argument for the reporter to cover it. You can increase your prospects for a successful pitch if you:

1. Always start by asking if this is a good time to talk. If the reporter is working on deadline, offer to call back later.

2. Pitch to reporters you know (and get to know lots of reporters). Remember the basics of developing relationships; journalists depend on sources they can trust for good information.

3. Incorporate the elements of newsworthiness in your pitch. Emphasize conflict, controversy, significance, and timeliness.

4. Give reasons why the story is timely *now*.

5. Broaden the base of the story. Think of why it might be important to people who drive, people concerned about their health, people with children—the broadest possible audience. The more people potentially affected, the better your story's prospects.

6. Pitch specific stories, not general issues. For example, don't talk about the problem of poverty but about specific policies that make the problem better or worse and specific people suffering or benefitting from those policies. Explain why these people's experience is representative.

7. Try to link your issue to some other issue in the news.

8. Don't overprepare—don't read your pitch from a script.

9. Remember that the person you pitch to may have to turn around and pitch it to his or her editor. Keep it simple and clear. Emphasize key points. For example:

> "More than 150 people will be rallying tomorrow to protest the reduced transit schedule. The transit authority cuts mean that all the people on the east side will no longer have bus service on weekends. People will not be able to get to work and will lose their jobs."

10. Don't be discouraged if the person is not interested in your story. You may have to pitch it to several different people.

Think about your pitch. Have you emphasized what's interesting? Can you describe the visuals that are part of the story? One long-time anchor explained that pitches are like home movies: The people making the pitch, like the ones showing the home movies, think it is great stuff, but the people watching the home movies often fall asleep. You must interest people outside your "family" if you want to have a successful pitch. (See *Try It Out* at the end of this chapter.)

ADVOCACY IN ACTION: Pesticides Pitch

We were talking to an expert on environmental health, to find out the latest issues related to environmental risks for children. She told us about new studies showing that environmental toxins affect the hormone systems of animals and that environmental toxins are likely endocrine disrupters for young children as well, because their forming physiology is so vulnerable. We asked about where the poisons were coming from, and one place she mentioned was pesticides, including pesticides in the home.

"Pesticides *in* the home?" we asked.

"Sure," she said. "Toxins like flea bombs leave residues that linger many days after the product has been used—in the air inside the home, and on children's toys, particularly stuffed animals."

We knew this would be a story. First, we were surprised, and we're public health professionals. If our interest was piqued, others' interest would be, too. Second, it's ironic: People are taking an action to remove a pest from their homes but may be causing a worse harm to their children in the process. Third, it affects thousands of homes and millions of children of all classes in all places, a broad audience. Fourth, a news story on this topic could really make a difference, by alerting parents to the dangers and giving them advice about how to avoid poisoning their children and by putting regulatory agencies and industry on notice. Finally, we could visualize the pictures: a room fogged up with flea bomb spray; small children crawling on the floor, putting toys in their mouths, hugging a stuffed panda close . . . dramatic images that would help make the story compelling.

To pitch the story, one of us e-mailed a health producer we know, who works for a major TV magazine news show: "Hey, I've got another story idea for you. Kids poisoned in their own homes by pesticides. Inside, not in the garden. Cuddled up to panda, who's been soaking up the flea bomb spray. Whatcha think?" The producer called within the hour, interested in the story.

When a Journalist Calls You . . .

When a reporter calls for a quote, many people's initial response is to try to please the reporter. You can do this, but also keep *your* goals—not just the reporter's—in mind. To get focused, start by asking the reporter a few questions about the story:

1. **What's your story?** This will tell you how the reporter is thinking about the story. Journalists may not know very much about the topic; TV reporters in particular often have to gather all the facts on a story in a single day. So the answer to this question tells you the reporter's "take" on the story and gives you an opportunity to respond; you can correct any misinformation or point out a more compelling angle on the story.

2. **How did you get my name?** If you don't already know the journalist, it helps to find out where he or she got your name. Whether he or she was referred by friend or foe will give you a sense of what he or she is expecting you to say.

Checklist: What to Ask When a Journalist Calls

- What's your story?
- How did you get my name?
- Who else have you talked to?
- What do you need?
- What's your deadline?

---

3. **Who else have you talked to?** This question also gives you the chance to find out how the story has been shaped so far. You may be able to suggest other people for the reporter to interview to help reinforce your perspective on the story. Also, you may not be the best person to be interviewed for the story, and you may be able to suggest someone more appropriate. You can also suggest specific questions for the reporter to ask of these sources.

4. **What do you need from me?** Sometimes, people get all geared up to return a reporter's call, thinking it will be an interview, when really the journalist just needs a key statistic or a referral to another person to interview. Be sure to ask what they need so you can give them the most complete information or referral. If they do need an interview, you can get a sense of what role you will play in the story: "I need to get your perspective as an opponent of this bill," or "I want to hear how the social service world is responding to the challenge of welfare reform."

5. **What's your deadline?** This is a critical question—it lets you know whether the reporter is rushing to make a broadcast in an hour or is preparing for a special feature to air next week. Then, you'll know whether you must act right away or whether you can take some additional time to collect your thoughts and develop a strategy before the interview.

After you've asked these questions, the ball is in your court. If you need time to collect your thoughts and frame your response, put the reporter on hold for a minute or ask to call back in a few minutes. If you are not the right person to answer the reporter's questions, decline the interview but be prepared for the reporter to pressure you by emphasizing the important things that you have to say. It helps if you can provide the name of someone else to be interviewed in your place.

If you go ahead with the interview, don't be so focused on meeting the reporter's needs that you stretch yourself beyond your limits. Always tell the truth. Never exaggerate. Never guess at the answer to a question. Do not compromise your credibility by talking about issues on which you are not adequately versed. Be honest, educate the journalist, and know your limits.

What will they ask me?

With a little thought, it is not difficult to predict what a reporter might want to know about an issue. Asking the questions above will help you ascertain what the journalist wants to know. In general, you can expect some form of the following two questions:

- What is the problem?
- What is the solution?

Your job is to connect those questions to your definitions of problem and solution. You can answer the same question many different ways, depending on what you strategically have decided to focus on in the interview. (See "Same Question, Different Answer" box on page 96.) Reporters will often be seeking the "human angle" of the story. Toward that end, they may ask you how you feel. Take the opportunity to tell them how you feel about policymakers' action or inaction on the issue, as opposed to just your personal emotional response.

Above all, remember: *Everything* is on the record. Even when you are talking casually over the phone. Even when you know the reporter as a personal friend. Even when the reporter says, "Tell me, off the record . . ." Never say anything to a reporter that you wouldn't want to see on the front page of the next day's newspaper or hear on the evening news. It's not that reporters are sneaky or untrustworthy; it's just their job to report the news—so don't give them anything you don't want them to report.

> **Rule 7:**
> *An interview is not a conversation.*

Interview Pointers and Pitfalls

Many people are extremely nervous about talking with journalists. Some caution and concern are healthy and can serve to keep you focused. However, too much can make you so anxious that you simply shut down. Here are some general points to keep in mind:

- **Journalists are after good material for a story.** They are not really interested in making you look good or bad. They are interested in telling the story.

- **Know your points well and be clear about your objectives for any particular interview.** Many people want to tell the journalist everything they know in a short interview. This is not only impossible but increases the likelihood that you will dilute the power of your message and squander the opportunity to advance your goals.

Same Question, Different Answer

The important thing when being interviewed is to keep focused on your goal. Here's an example of how the same question might be answered differently depending on what you ultimately want to achieve.

Question: Why do kids drink alcohol?

Goal: Restrict alcohol advertising that appeals to youth.

Answer: "Kids drink because everywhere they turn, attractive models are demonstrating that drinking is the way to have fun and be accepted. Kids need a fair chance. They need an environment that is not saturated with the wrong kind of alcohol messages 24 hours a day."

Goal: Increase local activities for teens.

Answer: "Kids are drinking because they have nothing better to do. The Teen Program we want to start would give kids a place to go and things to do, including the adult contact that makes a difference in young people's lives."

Goal: Eliminate fake IDs.

Answer: "Kids drink because it is too easy for them to get fake IDs and buy alcohol. We need uniform, unalterable identification to prohibit the proliferation of fake IDs."

Goal: Reduce access by raising the excise tax.

Answer: "Kids drink because alcohol is cheap and easy to get. A six-pack of beer should not cost the same as a six-pack of soda. If we raise the tax on beer just a nickel a drink, we would see a rapid drop in fatalities and injuries due to drinking and driving."

Of course, kids drink alcohol for all these reasons, and others. Strategically, you choose to emphasize the reason that will help underscore your proposed policy solution.

- **You are the expert.** In most cases, the journalist has limited expertise on the topic and may have just been handed the story that morning. Despite this, many people are intimidated by journalists, somehow believing that the reporter is more knowledgeable than they. Don't forget that you are the expert and that is why the journalist is talking with you.

- **An interview is not a conversation.** In a conversation, it is easy to get drawn off your main point or even forget where you started. In an interview, you must know the point you want to make.

Journalists make their living by talking with people. However, they are usually looking for specific kinds of information. They might ask you the same question two, three, or even four times to get an answer in a format they can use. You, as someone with a specific point to get across, might answer different questions with the same answer. In other words, both you and the journalist act in a manner that is specific and purposeful, in a way that conversations are not.

There are four pitfalls that you must avoid to be successful in meeting your interview objectives.

1. **You say too much.** You make your point and then keep going, saying something you hadn't intended to say or making a lesser point than your main one. Inevitably, it seems, it is this lesser point that ends up getting used.

Solution: Practice what to say—and when to stop.

2. **You stray from your area of expertise.** Under pressure from the reporter to give an opinion or fact in an area with which you are not familiar, you say something that is inaccurate. This ends up getting quoted, and you get in trouble with your colleagues or, worse, lose credibility with the journalist when he or she finds out the information is incorrect.

Solution: Don't be afraid to say "I don't know." Offer to find out the answer or put the reporter in contact with someone who does know.

3. **You relax too much.** You are having a nice conversation with a reporter and provide some information that you did not want to become public.

Solution: Maintain a professional distance in interviews, and always keep your objective in mind. Be pleasant but do not allow yourself to become too comfortable or relaxed.

4. **You fill the gap.** You've just answered a question, and there is a pause. Rather than waiting for the next question, you fill the gap and provide additional information that you had not intended to give out.

Solution: Don't be afraid of silence. If you feel compelled to fill the gap, you should simply restate your main point. You can also fill a long silence by asking the reporter if you've answered the question, or ask if she or he has any more questions. During phone interviews, understand that the reporter needs time to take down your answers before asking another question. Rather than being thrown off by the silence, use the time to collect your own thoughts.

If you decide to do an interview, it should be because it meets some specific objective. It may be to advance a specific policy issue, communicate a point directly to a specific influential target, develop a relationship with an important reporter, or simply to get some more experience being interviewed. Once you decide to do the interview, you should be very clear about the specific point you want to make and how you want to support that point.

Live Broadcast Interviews

You may get an opportunity to be interviewed live, either on TV or radio. This is a special challenge because you have to be especially focused and determined to convey your perspective clearly in a live broadcast interview. A few tips to make it work:

1. **Develop a file of arguments and counterarguments** on your issue and practice them in advance with your colleagues and with friends or family who are not familiar with your work. The object is to express yourself simply.

2. **Arrive at the interview location early** so that you have time to look around and check out the environment. Ask what the first question will be, and then think about how to use that question to get to your key point. Have your initial response thought out and ready. However, you cannot rely on the first question being what the interviewer told you it would be.

3. **Present the problem and your solution concisely.** You need to be able to tell your story clearly and succinctly. "Live on-air time" seems to move a lot faster than real time, so make your point early and often. Otherwise, you may hear, "We're out of time, thank you for coming today," just as you are getting ready to deliver your best media bite.

4. **Have several media bites ready.** Avoid jargon, technical terms, and acronyms. Too often advocates speak in a professional or cultural code that is not clear to journalists or the general public.

5. **Have your "bottom line" message prepared** to bail you out in case of trouble. Laurie Leiber, a prominent advocate for alcohol advertising controls, is frequently questioned about controversial and complex First Amendment issues that divert attention from the problem of alcohol advertising's influence on children. To turn the conversation back to the key point, she often says, "Look, we're talking about the number one drug problem among American youth."

ADVOCACY IN ACTION: Preparing for a Live Interview

One of the authors, Lawrence Wallack, was asked one day to come to the TV studio for a live interview on the six o'clock news concerning college student drinking. A new study had been released on binge drinking on college campuses, and the television medical reporter was quite concerned about the topic. Wallack was asked to do the interview because of his relationship with the medical reporter and her producer and his high profile on alcohol issues generally, but he felt hesitant because he felt he did not know a great deal about the specific topic. He ultimately agreed to do it as an opportunity to help advance some policy issues.

He immediately called several people with much more expertise on the topic than he and obtained the latest information on policy approaches to college drinking. As a result of these calls, he decided to focus on the issue of alcohol availability around the college campus area, drawing attention to the number of alcohol outlets and special promotions using cheap drinks to get students into the bars.

He also prepared to answer some predictable questions, including "What can parents do to help keep their kids safe from alcohol problems on campus?" He wanted to focus not on the traditional messages of communication between parents and kids but on what parents could do as advocates to help change the alcohol environment around campuses.

By the time he got to the television station, he knew exactly what he wanted to say and was able to communicate it clearly. After talking about the policy issues of alcohol availability on campus, he was asked the anticipated question about what parents could do. Wallack said,

> Parents have to check out what the college is doing to limit the easy availability of cheap alcohol on and around campus. Every [college] administrator knows that alcohol is the No. 1 problem on campus, and they have to deliver to parents, to tell them what they're going to do to help their children be safe on campus and reach their full educational potential.

Wallack was able to achieve his goal of focusing on the environment within which drinking takes place, rather than on the personal behavior of the students.

When You're on the Defensive

Sometimes, when reporters come knocking, it's not so welcome. When the executive director of your public service agency has been caught with his hand in the till or the celebrity who has worked so tirelessly for your animal rights cause appears on national TV in a fur coat, the media spotlight may suddenly be on you—and you're on the defensive. In a crisis situation,

1. **Try to stay calm and be courteous.** Explosive language and excessive emotion make for good news coverage; in this case, you don't want that.

2. **Never exaggerate, evade, or lie.** Your credibility is your only currency with reporters, and if you squander it in a crisis, you'll never restore their faith.

3. **Never say "No comment."** Remember you can put a reporter on hold to collect your thoughts. If you must, tell him or her you are still sorting out the facts of the case, but be sure to get back quickly with a statement. Try to make someone available to respond to questions at all times.

4. **Plan for a crisis in advance.** Anticipate tough questions that might be asked and practice answering them. Decide ahead of time who appropriate spokespeople will be and who should not speak to the media. Some organizations have been damaged by well-meaning employees who are cornered by reporters and asked to comment on a crisis case; if you decide a single designated spokesperson should respond to all media inquiries in a crisis (a good idea), communicate this to your staff in advance.

Suppose a journalist asks, "We've learned that your community organizer has a criminal record and has served time for assault. Is it appropriate to have such a person working at a child abuse agency?" You probably don't want to discuss the case in any way or respond to the question directly. How do you answer? Test out some transitions with your staff. For example, you can say to the journalist, "I'm sorry, but you know we can't discuss personnel issues. However, each of our staff is fully qualified in his or her areas.

Above all, realize that this too shall pass. Long after the specifics of this crisis have faded from reporters' memories, what they will still remember is the way you handled the heat of the moment. Your long-term relationship with reporters is usually more important than any passing crisis, so do your best to impress them with your straightforward, sincere response to the crisis.

Anticipating Arguments and Answering Tough Questions

Anticipate challenging questions in advance; the last thing you want is to hear a difficult question for the first time in the heat of an interview.

Advocates are generally expert at arguing their issues. However, sometimes they don't give enough attention to anticipating the arguments of the opposition. This is important because you may have to respond to these questions in a debate format, or you may hear the question from a journalist. After all, it is likely that the other side will suggest to the journalist, "You should really ask her how they reconcile the mayor's report saying their plan would bankrupt the city."

How can you anticipate all the difficult questions? Well, you can probably never predict all of them. However, there are things that you can do to minimize the likelihood of being in such an uncomfortable situation. We suggest you put together your list of the most difficult questions you "never want to be asked" and then prepare to answer them. Some of these, you can come up with from experience. We all can remember questions we heard being asked of colleagues and thought, "I'm glad I don't have to answer that."

Another source is asking friends and colleagues to come up with hard questions for you. No issue is airtight, and people can usually find the holes if they think about it. One of the best places we have found for identifying counterarguments to our points is on the editorial pages. Letters to the editor can be mined for the toughest questions; read all the letters opposing your position and challenge yourself to respond to the arguments the letter writers put forward. Between these voices from the community, editorials, and op-ed pieces, you can quickly develop your list of tough questions.

Once you've got your list of questions, you need to work on short, punchy responses. No matter how ridiculous you think the argument is on the other side, try to be prepared to respond to it. You will need some help in doing this, so do some role playing with your coworkers. Take turns trying to answer the questions. This is fun and also very productive practice.

ADVOCACY IN ACTION: Anticipating the Opposition's Arguments

In preparation for a meeting of gun policy advocates we were asked to put together a list of the most difficult questions on the topic of gun control. We reviewed the letters to the editor pages of major newspapers and found a great many challenging arguments against gun control. Based on our review, we presented the group with a list of the toughest questions (without answers). The experts agreed that virtually every question they were concerned about was on our list, and they used the meeting to develop responses.

Using Pivot Phrases

Some questions may distract you from your key messages. This is when you should remember that you don't have to answer every question literally. For instance, we once worked with a group promoting job training opportunities for young people. In a mock interview, we asked them, "Are our schools failing to prepare students for work, or are young people just not trying hard enough to find good jobs?" Because none of the advocates wanted to lay the blame on young people, they all started trying to describe what schools could do to improve. After struggling with her answer for awhile, one person finally blurted out in frustration, "Why did you ask us about schools? We're not working on schools." Our response was, "Then why did you start talking about schools?"

The lesson is, you can't control what you are asked; you can only control how you answer. It's a good idea to work on some quick transitions away from your problem questions. We call these pivot phrases. For example, when asked "Are our schools failing to prepare students for work, or are young people just not trying hard enough to find good jobs?," our advocate friend could have responded, "Neither one of those is what's most important. Let me tell you what is."

In another example, a reporter may present you with a very compelling personal story illustrating the opposite side of your argument; you can respond with, "Well, that's a tragic story, but it's just not typical. Let me tell you a more typical story." Some additional examples are shown on page 102.

You can't control what you are asked; you can only control how you answer.

Pivot Phrases in Action

You are asked:	*You answer:*
How do you feel about your personal tragedy?	I feel angry that [your target] hasn't taken steps to prevent this kind of tragedy from happening to others. [Go on to your policy solution.]
Isn't it really the parents' responsibility to worry about this problem facing young people?	Sure, parents are responsible, but parents need help. [Go on to your policy solution.]
What do you say to critics who say that if Joe Smith can overcome this problem without government support, so should everyone?	Well, Joe's story is very tragic (or compelling), but it's just not typical. Let me tell you a more typical story. [End up with your policy solution.]
Are our schools failing to prepare students for work, or are young people just not trying hard enough to find good jobs? [Or any other question where you're presented with two equally bad options.]	Actually, neither one of those is what's most important here. Let me tell you what is. [Go on to your policy solution.]
It must be very hard for you to get things done on this issue when your organization is the only one in the coalition that's willing to take a stand. [Or any other criticism or damaging question draped in the sheep's clothing of a sympathetic approach.]	Actually, our whole coalition is standing together on this issue, and we all feel that . . . [Go on to your policy solution.]

Summary Our seventh rule is: **An interview is not a conversation.** Talking to journalists is always a purposeful activity. You must always know why you are doing the interview and what point you want to make to support your policy objective. In an interview, unlike a conversation, you may repeatedly make the same point, tactfully ignore some questions, and most important, never really relax.

You can count on journalists asking at least two questions: What is the problem, and what do you want to see happen? You must be prepared to move quickly from the problem to your solution. Generally, people get into trouble with interviews when they say too much or offer opinions on topics that are not in their area of expertise. Assume that everything is on the record, and never lie or do anything to compromise your credibility.

TRY IT OUT: PITCHING WORKSHEET

Reporters don't have as much time as they used to for "hanging out" in the neighborhoods to find good stories. These days, they must rely on what others bring to their attention. When you have a good story, use this worksheet to prepare to tell a journalist about it. Remember, when you call a journalist to pitch a story, you are not asking for a favor. Rather, you are alerting him or her to a compelling story, thus helping reporters do their job, which is to report the news.

1. Before you call, fill out all the aspects of the story you want to pitch. You can use these questions as a starting point.

    What is going to happen? _____
    Why is it interesting or important (newsworthy)? _____
    Who is the story about? _____
    Where and when is it going to happen? _____

2. Figure out what you want to say. Emphasize the different aspects of newsworthiness that might apply. Be sure to include a description of any visuals.

3. Ask a friend or coworker to help you practice your pitch.

4. Decide whom to call. Is this a story that suits newspapers, radio, or TV? If it is for TV, what will the pictures be?

5. When you call, ask if this is a good time. You can say, "I have a story I thought you might be interested in—are you on deadline?" Be prepared to give a quick pitch right then. The reporter may want to hear a little bit before deciding whether to hear more.

6. Be prepared to pitch to voice mail—give a brief description of the story or event and leave your number to be contacted for more information.

7

EDITORIAL PAGE STRATEGIES

In this space, thoughts fly. Views are expressed. Visions unfurl . . . It is this page that policymakers look at first, along with captains of industry, masters of the arts, and many of the great thinkers of this generation.

Advertisement for buying space on the Op-Ed page of The New York Times

---

After the front page, the most frequently read section of the newspaper is the editorial page. In fact, this page is probably your best chance to present an extended argument to reach the decision makers you are targeting. With editorials by newspaper staff, letters by readers, and columns and op-ed pieces by both professional writers and community members, this is the place where policymakers turn to quickly assess what the hot issues are among their constituents. One staff member for a state legislator told us that the first task of the district office each morning is to fax to the capitol office the front pages and editorial pages of all the local newspapers, so the legislator can keep abreast of key issues in the community.

The opinion pages provide a great opportunity for advocates. There, you can make a quick point and keep an issue alive. Writing an op-ed piece, letter, or even a paid editorial advertisement that runs on the op-ed page are all good ways to focus your ideas and sharpen your points. If your opinion piece is published, you can turn it into "news you can re-use" by copying the printed piece and distributing it to others. Send copies to your supporters to reinforce their work and provide them with your best arguments. Pass it along to funders so they are aware of your leadership and initiative on the issue. And, be sure to send copies to all the key opinion leaders and policymakers you are trying to sway on this issue. Having your ideas and name published provides status and credibility for you and your issue.

> ## Rule 8:
> *Use the opinion pages to reach policymakers and opinion leaders.*

In his book, *Behind the Oval Office,* Dick Morris noted that if you want to reach President Clinton, op-ed pages are a good bet:

> Clinton did read magazines and op-ed articles regularly. If you wanted your views to reach the president, the way to do it was through the op-ed pages of *The New York Times* and the *Washington Post* or through articles in *Harper's, The New Yorker,* the *New Republic,* the *Atlantic,* and a few other magazines.[1]

Morris wasn't kidding about reaching the president through the op-ed pages. A 1997 front-page story in *The New York Times* discussed high-tech devices that police can use to spot people carrying concealed guns. The idea had appeared in a *New York Times* op-ed piece three years earlier, which President Clinton had read. According to the article, he then "pushed the Justice Department to begin financing the research program for anti-crime technology. The new devices are the first fruits of this project, Justice Department officials say."[2]

ADVOCACY IN ACTION: Extending a Story Through the Op-Ed Pages

In December 1997, a 14-year-old in Kentucky drew a handgun from his backpack and shot several classmates, killing three and wounding five others. The story made front-page headlines but might have faded away quickly in places outside of Kentucky if not for advocates extending the story by writing letters to the editor. One group in Orange County, California, generated several letters on policies needed to keep guns out of the hands of children; they also wrote back when their ideas were criticized in letters by pro-gun advocates. That month, the *Orange County Register* reported that the debate over gun policies was the No. 1 topic on its letters to the editor page. The advocates were able to keep the issue on the agenda and expand the coverage well beyond the original news event that inspired the letters in the first place.

Writing Op-Ed Pieces and Commentaries

An op-ed piece gives you an opportunity to expand on your ideas, tell a personal story, or give the background on your issue. You can reach decision makers without having to rely on a reporter to translate your ideas for you.

Because these pages are so popular, it can be extremely difficult to get an op-ed piece published. The *San Francisco Chronicle,* for example, gets 50 op-ed submissions a day and can only publish one or two. Dean Wakefield, opinion pages editor for that paper, recommends that people submitting op-ed pieces "don't write too much—650-700 words max. I don't have time to cut."[3] Wakefield notes that he likes to print pieces that are related to breaking news when he can. Although he welcomes submissions from everyone, he especially wants more material from "real people—everyday people, not professional PR types. I want it personalized. Make the issue real to readers."[4]

When you write your op-ed piece, the same tenets of newsworthiness apply as when you try to pitch a news event. Your piece is more likely to be published if it relates to a hot news topic, details a controversy or conflict in the community, tells a personal story, or relates to a significant anniversary or milestone. In this setting, you can make effective use of creative writing techniques such as metaphors, personal voice, and quotes from literature or historical figures. Be impassioned and write from the heart; that will give your piece the real flavor that will set it apart from the many PR-generated drafts submitted to papers every day.

Some further tips for writing a successful op-ed piece:

- Call the newspaper and find out the range of words they accept for consideration. Most papers like between 600 and 800 words, but sometimes formats for up to 1,200 words are available. Also ask whether the editors prefer submissions via e-mail or fax.

- Read the op-ed pieces published by the paper to get a sense of the style they like. Pay attention to whether they have published other op-ed pieces on your issue recently.

- Make sure you have something different to say.

- Develop one idea and support it with concrete examples, tell personal stories when possible, and provide a conclusion regarding what you want to happen.

- You can pitch your idea to the editor before you send it in, or you can just send it "cold." We suggest that if you choose to pitch in advance, write the piece before you call so you know you can deliver. When you are ready, e-mail or fax it in and then call with a clear explanation of the importance of your topic. Be sure to mention how your piece relates to breaking news. (See *Try It Out* at the end of this chapter.)

Radio Commentaries

In addition to the op-ed pages, there is another way to editorialize—on the radio waves. Many radio stations, especially public radio, accept commentaries from listeners and may be especially interested in perspectives from young people. The elements of a commentary are similar to those of an op-ed piece. Call the radio station you listen to and ask what its process is for accepting listener commentaries. Some may ask to see a script of your remarks in advance. Be sure to ask how long your commentary should be (usually 30 to 60 seconds), and be sure that your script fits in that time if you read it slowly and clearly. Most stations will ask you to come into the studio to record the piece, so it will sound clear and professional.

You will not have control over when your radio commentary is aired, but the advantage is that many stations play each commentary several times. This may be a good way to expand the reach of your viewpoints or reach a different audience than with a written op-ed piece. (See *Try It Out* at the end of this chapter.)

ADVOCACY IN ACTION: Changing Policy Through an Op-Ed Piece

In Louisiana, alcohol policy advocates had long been concerned about drinking among underage youth. Although federal law mandated a minimum legal drinking age of 21 years, a loophole in Louisiana law made the drinking age virtually unenforceable: It was not illegal for vendors to sell alcohol to 18- to 20-year-olds. This effectively amounted to a drinking age of 18.

In 1996, based on concern about alcohol's role in traffic fatalities among youth, the state made it illegal for alcohol to be sold to anyone under 21. However, lawyers for the alcohol industry succeeded in overturning the law on appeal, by presenting data showing that the total number of crashes among 21- to 23-year-olds was slightly greater than the total number of crashes among 18- to 20-year-olds. "The industry claimed that these raw numbers showed the older group was more 'responsible' for alcohol-related fatalities, and therefore the law arbitrarily discriminated against 18- to 20-year-olds," said Richard Scribner, MD, a medical professor at Louisiana State University and advocate for the higher drinking age.

Scribner could demonstrate that the state Supreme Court had made a mistake in ruling on the basis of raw data, because it failed to take into account that there are many more older drivers overall than 18- to 20-year-old drivers. "It's like saying motorcycles have fewer crashes than cars, so it must be safer to drive a motorcycle," Scribner said.

Unfortunately, the state's lawyers could not present these data directly to the court because the court had refused to consider any new evidence. "The only way to get the high court to hear it was to get it into the newspaper," Scribner said. He wrote an op-ed piece explaining how younger drivers are at higher risk from alcohol-related crashes—the odds of a fatal crash are much greater for the 18- to 20-year-old age group, even though they have fewer such crashes overall—and calling on the Supreme Court to therefore protect younger drivers by allowing legislation that would reduce their drinking. He sent it to several newspapers in the state and followed up particularly with the newspaper that served the home district for the Supreme Court Justice who opposed the higher drinking age.

Ultimately the court did reverse its decision and raised the drinking age to 21. In doing so, the ruling explicitly acknowledged that the court had earlier erred in not considering crashes by percentage of licensed drivers. "This was precisely my point in the op-ed," Scribner noted, "and I'm certain we could not have gotten the court's attention in any other way."[5]

Writing Letters to the Editor

Letters to the editor provide a useful and visible forum for community members to express their perspectives on current events. One researcher notes that "surveys consistently show that letters are among the best-read parts of the paper."[6] Letters to the editor can signal community interest in an issue and send a message to policymakers.

Letters to the editor should be short and punchy, and if the letter is in direct response to a news story, you should respond quickly. Try to generate several letters from your friends and colleagues because the number of letters will signal the importance of the topic and increase the likelihood that at least one letter will be published.

As with other media strategies, always keep your objective in mind. It can be tempting to respond in anger to an article or column you find particularly idiotic; just be sure you know what your purpose is. What would you like readers to do, what solutions would you like them to support, as a result of reading your letter?

When writing a letter to the editor of a newspaper or magazine, keep the following tips in mind:

What would you like readers to do, what solutions would you like them to support, as a result of reading your letter?

• **Respond quickly.** If you see something in the paper that you want to respond to, try to send your letter (by e-mail or fax) by the next day, at the latest.

• **Mention your reason for writing,** preferably in the first sentence. If you are responding directly to an article you read in the publication, state the article's headline and publication date. If you are commenting on a local current event, be specific about the issue or event.

• **Limit the content to one or two key points.** A letter to the editor offers the chance for a concise statement on a subject, not an in-depth analysis. Focus on the one message you want readers to get from your letter.

• **Take a strong position.** Letters Section editors look for fresh facts, honest statements of opinion, and creative slants on the news. If you can, use a compelling fact that shows the urgency or importance of your issue. Include a call to action.

• **Keep your letter to three paragraphs.** Aim for about 250 words (200 words or less for some papers—check the letters section for limits for each paper). The more direct and simple your letter is, the more likely it will be published. Longer letters are often edited to make them shorter; don't leave the editing up to the editors, who may cut your most important point.

Here are basics to follow in preparing a submission. Start your letter with "Dear Editor." Include your name, address, and phone number; an editor may call you to verify that you wrote the letter. You may submit your letter on personal or professional letterhead, depending on what is most appropriate for the subject matter. (Bear in mind any organizational restrictions on making political endorsements.) To be sure your letter gets into the hands of the right editor, get the name of the Letters Section editor (listed on the masthead in most publications, or you can call and ask for the name of the person to whom you should mail, e-mail, or fax the letter). (See *Try It Out* at the end of this chapter.)

ADVOCACY IN ACTION: Letter on Sexually Transmitted Diseases

On March 9, 1998, a front-page story in *The New York Times* discussed the epidemic of sexually transmitted diseases. We had been working with the Centers for Disease Control to try to reframe public debate around this issue to reflect a series of policy recommendations that had come out in an Institute of Medicine (IOM) report almost 18 months earlier. *The Times* story was informative, but it did not include the policy issues mentioned in the IOM report. We decided to write a letter to the editor for several reasons:

- To praise the front-page story and note that it contributed to breaking the "conspiracy of silence" on the issue.
- To call attention to a missing a policy perspective and thus highlight the IOM recommendations.
- To emphasize the magnitude of the problem for youth (three million preventable infections were occurring every year).
- To provide a model to other advocates of one way they might enter their perspective in the public debate on this issue.

"Fighting Sexual Disease" was the only letter *The New York Times* published in response to the story. (See Figure 7.1.)

Fighting Sexual Disease

To the Editor:

Your March 9 front-page article on the epidemic of sexually transmitted diseases makes an important contribution to breaking what one expert calls the "conspiracy of silence." According to the Institute of Medicine, there are 12 million new infections every year, including about three million among adolescents. These infections are preventable.

Providing resources to address this problem may not poll as well as beating up the tobacco industry, but leaders must recognize the impact of S.T.D.'s on youth. Initiatives suggested by the Institute include sex education in schools, including access to condoms and clinical services, condom advertising, integration of treatment and prevention in health care, and making sure that the uninsured receive treatment and prevention services. It is hypocritical to blame young people for high S.T.D. rates when we do not provide the means for prevention.

LAWRENCE WALLACK
Berkeley, Calif., March 10, 1998

Figure 7.1.   A Letter to the Editor on Sexual Disease
SOURCE: *The New York Times.* (1998, March 14), Editorials & Letters. Copyright 1998, *The New York Times*, reprinted with permission.

ADVOCACY IN ACTION: Letter on Child Care

The National Institute of Child Health and Human Development (NICHHD) released a study showing that the mental and intellectual development of babies in day care was just as good as the development of children cared for by their mothers. The study was widely reported, including in the *Los Angeles Times.*

We had been working with a group of child care advocates and wanted to take advantage of the opportunity generated by the coverage of the NICHHD study. We wanted to use this opportunity to emphasize the importance of quality in child care and call for public subsidies of infant care in particular.

We wrote a letter that illustrated the high costs of infant care. It said, "The average cost of infant care . . . is $159 per week per baby. So with three infants, the average caregiver would take in less than $2,000 a month. That's hardly enough to live on, let alone to cover facilities costs, insurance, supplies, training, and the rest." We suggested that baby-kissing politicians should "put their money where their mouths are" and help share the costs of investing in quality child care. An edited version of the letter was printed in the *Los Angeles Times.* (See Figure 7.2.)

Quality Care for Children

Re "Study Says Day Care Affects Bonding but Not Learning," April 4: The latest study on child care has made it clear: Young children learn and grow when their caregivers give them plenty of attention and interaction—whether that caregiver is Mommy or a day care provider.

A key component of "quality" in child care is the number of children per caregiver. I'd say the reasonable limit is three babies per adult.

The average cost of infant care in my county, Alameda, is $159 per week per baby. So with three infants, the average caregiver would take in less than $2,000 a month. That's hardly enough to live on, let alone to cover facility costs, insurance, supplies, training and the rest.

Strapped parents can't afford to pay more for child care. And caregivers already live at the brink of poverty. Clearly, it's time for government and business to step up to bat and share the costs of this most essential investment.

Affording child care is no longer just a family issue, it's a political issue. We need to get serious about investing in quality child care if we are to have a healthy community and solid future.

KATIE WOODRUFF
Berkeley

Figure 7.2. A Letter to the Editor on Child Care
SOURCE: *Los Angeles Times.* (1997, April 9), Letters to the Times. Copyright *Los Angeles Times;* reprinted with permission.

ADVOCACY IN ACTION: Youth Getting Involved

Letters to the editor are a good way for young people to make their voices heard in the media. Papers may be particularly interested in perspectives from youth. In Sacramento, California, in 1996, there were more gun dealers than gas stations. Many of these so-called "kitchen-table" gun dealers operate out of homes in residential areas. They are a particular problem because their operations are largely unobservable and provide an opportunity for illegal firearm sales.

When the city council considered an ordinance limiting the number of gun dealers, young people wrote letters to the newspaper to express their views. In a letter to the *Sacramento Bee,* Adina Medina wrote,

This April I will be 19. A lot of young people my age have lost their lives to gun violence and will continue to do so until something is done about it. I know a lot about this issue because I know a lot of people who have been the victims. How many more lives will be lost because of gun violence? The longer the City Council delays the vote, the more lives will be lost. I will not vote for anyone who does not support this cause. (Letters to the *Sacramento Bee* [1996, February], copyright *The Sacramento Bee*; used with permission)

Her letter was published; later that year, the city council passed the gun measure.

ADVOCACY IN ACTION: Getting Attention With a Letter

In 1997, several public health groups were involved in negotiations with the tobacco companies to draft federal legislation that would settle all present and future tobacco litigation against the companies. Several public health groups, including the American Cancer Society and the American Heart Association, supported the idea of giving legal immunity to the tobacco companies in return for stronger national tobacco control policies, such as authority to regulate cigarettes and cigarette advertising. A number of other public health groups and advocates disapproved of this process, believing it was wrong to use the legal rights of American citizens as a bargaining chip to achieve public policy gains.

One such advocate, Michael Siegel, MD, an assistant professor at Boston University School of Public Health, wrote a letter to the editor of *USA Today* in which he spotlighted the position of the American Cancer Society and American Heart Association and called on them to discontinue their support of any legislation that would take away people's legal rights to hold the tobacco companies fully accountable for damages caused by their products.

Within two days, Siegel received a response from the son of the president of the American Cancer Society, who was shocked to see that the organization was actually willing to consider trading some form of immunity for tobacco companies for public policy gains. In reaching the president's son, who probably shared his feelings of dismay with his father, the letter potentially had a greater effect than if the American Cancer Society's president had read the letter directly.

In addition, Siegel received a phone call from the Association of Trial Lawyers of America, which went on to help him place a longer op-ed piece with the Knight-Ridder news service. They went on to work together on this issue, so the letter served as an organizing tool for advocates who opposed tobacco industry immunity.

As this example demonstrates, the most powerful effect of letters to the editor may be not in their directly convincing readers of a particular argument but in bringing an issue or perspective to the attention of key individuals.

Don't overlook editorials. Editorial boards often get ideas for the subjects of their editorials from community and professional groups, as well as government representatives, who meet with them to present their perspective on an issue.

Editorial boards vary considerably in terms of their composition. They may include from 2 to 15 or more people, including some or all of the following: the editorial page editor, the letters editor, the op-ed page editor, the managing editor, and the city news editor. Some editorial boards may have a representative from the community and various reporters. No matter who is part of the group, this is the body that decides what issues should be covered in the paper's editorials.

The goal of meeting with the editorial board is to get the paper to write an editorial supporting the policy or position of your group. If this is a strategy you choose to pursue, you can call your local paper and request to meet with the editorial board. When you call, be prepared to describe the issue you want to discuss, your group's position on it, and who will attend the meeting. It probably helps to write a letter describing the purpose of the meeting but be sure to follow up by phone. (See *Try It Out* at the end of this chapter.)

Prepare key points and facts in writing to leave with the board, but do not expect any commitments on the spot. Just think of this as an opportunity to educate these influential gatekeepers, regardless of what action they take in the near term.

Before the meeting

• **Review the paper's previous editorials on your issue, if any.** You may be able to search on-line versions of the newspaper for previously published editorials. Be prepared to tell the board what is new since the last time they editorialized on your issue, and why now is an important time for them to take a stand.

• **Decide who from your group will attend the meeting (no more than three or four people).** Editorial board members get a lot of requests for meetings; they are likely to give highest priority to people they consider to be significant community players or to have special experience with the issue. You will probably have better luck being granted a meeting if your team includes high-profile members such as an executive director of a major agency, the head of a community coalition that represents significant numbers of community members, the high school student body president, and so on.

• **Decide on the persuasive points you want to make.** Try to limit your points to three key facts or statements, and practice making your case. Decide which member of your team will make which points.

• **Brainstorm tough questions on your issue.** Part of the editorial board's job is to challenge your position; be prepared to counter any arguments.

- **Prepare materials to leave with the board after your meeting.** These should explain your position, provide facts on the issue, and contain a list of contacts for follow-up. (Ask your contact whether you should send these materials before the meeting.)

At the meeting

- **Introduce all members of your team,** and make sure you get the names and positions of all the editorial board members.

- **Strongly advocate your position.** Explain why an editorial would be timely and important now. Ask specifically for an editorial to support your position, but do not expect any assurances.

- **Have a backup plan.** If the board tells you during the meeting that they will *not* write an editorial on the issue, ask if they would print an op-ed piece written by a member of your team. Again, do not expect any commitments on the spot, but do get the name of the person to whom you should submit such a piece.

- **Be honest.** If you are asked something that you cannot answer, say that you do not know but will be happy to provide the information after the meeting is over.

- **Provide your key points and facts in writing.** Give the members the materials you've prepared for their review (described above).

After the meeting

- **Follow up with a phone call or note to your contact.** Thank him or her again for meeting with you, and use this opportunity to reiterate the importance of a timely editorial on the subject.

- **Honor commitments quickly.** If you promised any follow-up materials or information during the meeting, provide them promptly. If you floated the idea of an op-ed piece, draft it quickly, within the paper's word limits, and submit it to the appropriate person.

- **Protect your investment of time and effort.** Remember that even if you do not get an editorial at this time, the contacts you established with key editors will be invaluable in the future. Stay in touch with the editors through occasional phone calls or notes in which you provide additional information or perspectives.

ADVOCACY IN ACTION: Resources for Youth Editorial Board Visit

After participating in the Resources for Youth news conference described in Chapter 4, several advocates went to meet with the editorial board of the *Sacramento Bee* to ask them to editorialize in support of effective violence prevention programs in local communities. In the meeting, two pollsters presented the public opinion data, a community organizer talked about the impact these programs had on the people in his own neighborhood, and a policy expert described the specific pieces of legislation that would invest in specific programs across the state.

Significantly, although the polling data had been an important news hook for the press conference, the editorial board appeared less interested in them. To them, what was "fresh" about the group's presentation was the viewpoint of the community activist who attended, Bernardo Rosa. Rosa talked about how participating in the violence prevention initiative gave him and his community a voice and a new language for working for change. The editor commented that this was a perspective she hadn't expected to hear in the meeting, and the participants felt that without that balance in their group, she would not have taken their issue as seriously.

Although the paper did not run an editorial on the issue at that time, the advocates felt it was a successful meeting. They had educated key people at the *Bee* and laid a foundation for a continuing relationship. Rosa said, "Whether or not they write a piece, I think we opened their eyes about what these programs do for us at the community level. They needed to hear the truth, not just the sound bites."

Summary

Our eighth rule is: **Use the opinion pages to reach policymakers and opinion leaders.** The opinion pages are closely followed by influential targets and those whom you want to mobilize. Any overall strategy should include meeting with the editorial boards of newspapers and writing op-ed pieces and regular letters to the editor. Besides reaching people with whom you might not normally communicate, letters to the editor and op-ed pieces are products that you can use in several ways. They can be sent to members of your group or coalition, included in media packets, and mailed to legislators and others you want to educate on the issue. The editorial pages are high-credibility locations where your issue deserves to be placed.

Notes

1. Morris, D. (1997). *Behind the Oval Office.* New York: Random House, p. 99.

2. Butterfield, F. (1997, April 7). New devices may let police spot people on the street hiding guns. *New York Times,* p. A1.

3. Comments to *Mother Jones'* magazine's "Lunch Bunch" Journalist Speakers series, October 18, 1996.

4. Comments to *Mother Jones,* as above.

5. Personal communication, July 1998.

6. Rystrom, K. (1993). *The why, who and how of the editorial page* (2nd ed.). State College, PA: Strata Publishing Co., p. 247.

TRY IT OUT: PLANNING AN OP-ED PIECE OR COMMENTARY

Use the following questions to organize your thoughts about a potential op-ed piece or commentary you would like to write. After making your notes, it may be helpful to write without stopping or editing for several minutes to get your thoughts flowing. Then you can begin to shape a first draft.

What is the subject I would like to cover in my op-ed piece? _____

_____

What personal stories or examples can I give to illustrate why this problem is important? _____

_____

What is the specific policy solution I am advocating? _____

_____

What two or three key points would help convince people that this is the right action to take now?

_____

_____

What compelling facts or statistics could help make my case? _____

_____

What metaphors or images might help reinforce the point? _____

_____

TRY IT OUT: RADIO COMMENTARY PLANNING WORKSHEET

Many radio stations accept commentaries from listeners and may be especially interested in perspectives from young people. Call the radio station you listen to and ask what their process is for accepting listener commentaries. Some may ask to see a script of your remarks in advance. Be sure to ask how long your commentary should be (usually 30 to 60 seconds), and be sure that your script fits in that time if you read it slowly and clearly. Here are some questions you can use to plan your commentary; you can also use these points to plan what to say when you call in to a talk radio show:

The specific issue I am concerned about is _____

I have a unique perspective on this problem because _____

A story about my experience with this issue is _____

What many people don't realize is _____

One thing that could really make a difference is _____

TRY IT OUT: LETTER TO THE EDITOR WORKSHEET

Here is a sample letter to the editor format that may help you organize your ideas. You can use some or all of these sentence ideas in your letter, but try to use your own language as much as possible.

Letters to the Editor
[Newspaper name]
[Newspaper address, fax or email]

Date

Dear Editor:

Yesterday, you reported that _____.
This is [timely/interesting/ironic] because _____.
As a [parent/teacher/physician/community member/voter], my perspective is _____.
What people don't realize is _____.
One thing that could really make a difference is _____.

Sincerely,
[Signature]
[Your name, address, and phone number]

TRY IT OUT: EDITORIAL BOARD MEETING PLANNING WORKSHEET

Before you set up a meeting with an editorial board, it is a good idea to plan what you want to say about why the board should meet with your group. Editorial boards typically get many more requests for meetings than they can fulfill, so you should be prepared to make the strongest case possible for your issue. Use the following questions to focus your thoughts and draft a letter describing your group's objectives.

Newspaper we want to meet with:
Contact person for editorial board meetings:
Phone number/address:

Dear [Name]:

We would like to meet with your editorial board to discuss an issue of great importance for your readers. We are a coalition of _____ working to _____. Our coalition includes [list type of participants or number of community members represented].

_____

_____

The specific issue we would like to discuss with you is _____.
This is an important issue in general because _____.
It is particularly urgent/timely for your paper to take a stand on this issue on at this time because

_____.

We would be happy to provide you with additional material on this issue. We look forward to hearing from you soon about when we can meet.

Sincerely,
[Your name, address, and phone number]

OTHER MEDIA STRATEGIES
Paid Advertising, Talk Radio, and the Internet

---◆---

It's not about reaching everybody. It's about targeting the few who can make a difference. It's about starting a chain reaction. It's about getting to critical mass.

Herb Chao Gunther, Public Media Center

---◆---

Don't overlook other very powerful media access strategies: paid advertising, talk radio, and the Internet. This chapter discusses what to expect from each of these outlets, when it might be appropriate to use them, and how to increase your chances of success with these approaches.

> **Rule 9:**
> *Consider all kinds of media in your strategy.*

Sometimes advocates find that the best way to have ultimate control over the content and timing of their media messages is to buy advertising space. This allows you to target a specific message very narrowly. For instance, a group trying to pressure a few key senators might run an editorial-type advertisement to appear on the op-ed pages of the *Washington Post* or in the local newspapers of the targeted senators' states the day before a critical Senate vote. The op-ed

Put Your Dollars to Work: Paid Advertising

pages can be a particularly powerful place to run your paid advertisement and help make certain that your target receives your message.

Design a paid advertising campaign with the express intent of generating news coverage of the campaign.

Often, however, the benefits of paid advertising may be outweighed by the cost and limited reach of such ads and by the fact that advertisements inherently do not convey the same external sense of legitimacy as news coverage does. However, one useful strategy employed by some media advocates is to design a paid advertising campaign with the express intent of generating news coverage of the campaign. This leverages a limited amount of paid media into a much larger *earned media* splash.

For example, the Dangerous Promises coalition, which attempted to get beer companies to stop using sexist portrayals of women in their alcohol ads, developed controversial counterads that played off popular themes in beer advertisements. The local billboard companies in both Los Angeles and San Francisco declined to accept the ads, despite the fact that the coalition was not asking for public service space but had money to pay for the billboards. The fact that a coalition of nonprofit agencies was denied the right to buy space for two small antiviolence advertisements, whereas alcohol companies spend more than $2 billion a year to promote their products, created irony that helped make the story newsworthy.

For most advocates, the use of a paid advertisement may seem like a luxury that will forever be beyond their reach. However, in recent years, as funders and private donors become increasingly sophisticated about the importance of paid advertising, we are seeing much more of it. Sometimes, paid advertisements are purchased with funds from people who wish to have their name appear in the ad. Other times, a private donor may simply provide the resources to run an ad.

When deciding where to place your ad, bear in mind that radio ads can be narrowly targeted and relatively inexpensive. Tony Schwartz, a longtime guerrilla media activist who has made hundreds of ads, explains that all you really need for a radio ad is a good quality tape recorder and a professional voice. Buying time for the ad during "drive time"—the morning or afternoon commute—can ensure that your message reaches the person you want to talk to. Even if the specific person does not happen to hear the ad during their commute, you can be reasonably sure that when he or she reaches the office, there will be a message from someone who had heard the ad and wants to know what it was all about.

A cheaper alternative to mainstream media ad buys, if it makes sense for your target audience, is to advertise on the Internet. An Internet newsletter explained how the environmental group, Friends of the Earth (FOE), ran ads on various search engines to reach people who were using the Internet to get purchase information on sport utility vehicles. The goal of FOE was to get the web surfers to go to the FOE web page and read about how these vehicles contribute to environmental problems.

Internet advertising is still a very narrow field, however, compared with the ability to focus and target specific audiences through mainstream media advertisements. In sum, designing and purchasing advertising is a significant decision because it can be a substantial investment of limited resources, will increase the visibility of the issue and your group, may be very controversial, and could generate some backlash. It is very important to remember the purpose of the ad and how it fits in with your larger strategy. Some important benefits of paid advertising include the following:

- increase visibility and credibility of your issue and organization;
- reinforce the efforts of advocates in the field and boost morale;
- generate news stories to advance the issue;
- reach key decision makers in a timely way;
- implement a shaming strategy by amplifying your side of the conversation with a specific official or organization so the community hears it;
- state your position directly and have total control over the way your statement is conveyed.

If you're going to pay for placement for an advertisement, make sure you do it well to get the most out of your investment.

**Paid Media:
Tips for Success**

Create ad copy that reads easily This is not a policy paper. Most readers will skim the ad for the main points. Keep sentences short. And tell the story: Who is affected? Why is it such a serious problem? What can be done about it? Who has to do it?

Use visuals to draw attention. The ad should catch the reader's eye. You can do this with photographs (for example, show a photo of the mayor or other target, the smokestack polluting the neighborhood, a family or person affected by the problem). You can generally get photos of public figures such as politicians or executives from their public relations offices. Get written permission to use photos of private individuals, such as people affected by the problem.

Point a finger. Clearly define the person or institution that has the power to make the change, as well as the action that needs to be taken.

Make it easy to act. Give readers an opportunity to respond. Include a telephone number to call and a coupon that readers can send to the target, demanding action, or to your organization to join, donate, or get more information.

Give information, not just slogans. Paid ads give you a platform to empower people with real information. Give your readers the facts surrounding the issue and make it relevant to their lives. Use polls, surveys, or studies to demonstrate your point and show the extent of the problem.

Be accurate. If members of the opposition find an inaccuracy in your ad, they will try to exploit it and portray you as dishonest. Make sure your numbers and facts are correct and that you can back them up.

Checklist: How to Create and Place a Paid Print Ad

- Call the newspaper, radio station, or TV station and find out the costs for placing ads. Ask about discounts for nonprofit groups. Find out the deadlines and design requirements for the ad (size, length, etc.).
- Find out if the news outlet has legal requirements regarding ad content.
- Brainstorm headlines that will draw the reader into the ad; develop visuals or select photos to include.
- If you are placing a newspaper ad, aim for a half- or full-page ad or for space on the op-ed page—a section that most policymakers pay attention to. Small, quarter-page ads in other sections of the paper tend to get lost and are not usually worth the expense.
- Gather signers to the ad to give your objective more legitimacy. This is your chance to demonstrate widespread and influential support for your position.
- Work with a designer to create a simple, interesting design that looks professional.

Time your placement well. Place your ad at a strategic time—during a meeting of industry representatives in your area, a vote at the public health commission, a shareholders' meeting, or an anniversary relevant to your issue. This will increase the impact of your ad and may spin off into free media coverage. Often, journalists will cover such events, and your ad might contribute another perspective to the debate or force the decision makers to answer the questions raised by your ad.

ADVOCACY IN ACTION: An Ad to Create Public Pressure and Build Legitimacy

In April 1998, a coalition seeking to stop Anheuser Busch from using cartoonlike characters in their advertising took out a half-page ad immediately prior to the company's annual shareholders' meeting. The ad depicted the many animated "spokescharacters" Anheuser Busch has employed over the years, from Spuds McKenzie to the Bud Frogs and Bud Lizards, and called on stockholders to support a resolution ending beer advertising that appeals to children. (See Figure 8.1.) The ad was run in the *St. Louis Post Dispatch,* the hometown newspaper of the company, and the *Washington Post,* one of the important agenda-setting papers in the country. The advocates hoped that the ad would do a number of things:

- Create some controversy that would contribute to more news coverage than the issue might have otherwise received
- Energize advocates working on the issue who would see the ad or read about it in the news
- Apply pressure to the management of Anheuser Busch by shaming them through the ad
- Increase stockholder support for limits on advertising directed toward youth
- Alert members of Congress that many groups were concerned about this issue

The ad did accomplish some important objectives, including stimulating a news article in the *Wall Street Journal.* It helped convey the idea that "the Bud Frogs are to beer as Joe Camel is to cigarettes," as one advocate said. It also helped increase the credibility and legitimacy of the campaign. However, advocates involved in the campaign warned against seeing such a paid ad and the surrounding media splash as an end in itself. As with any media approach, a paid ad should be one tactic in your overall plan for advancing the policy goal; don't neglect the important tasks of organizing and mobilizing in the glare of the media spotlight.

Figure 8.1. An Example of a Paid Ad

SOURCE: Produced by the Marin Institute for the Prevention of Alcohol and Other Drug Problems for the 1998 campaign for childproof beer ads.

ADVOCACY IN ACTION: An Ad That Never Even Had to Be Played

In 1996, a California state legislator introduced legislation dubbed "the deadbeat dad relief act"—a bill that would dramatically reduce the amount of child support the state would be required to collect from parents who had missed child support payments. When the bill was debated, California had the worst child support collection record in the country, collecting payments for just 13% of the caseload. Failure to collect child support is a leading cause of child poverty and welfare dependence.

Advocates involved in Public Media Center's Child Support Reform Initiative created a radio ad to call attention to the deadbeat dad relief act and put legislators on notice that if they supported the measure to cut child support, they would be publicly shamed in future ad campaigns. The Initiative sent the radio ad copy to key legislators prior to buying any air time. Just the prospect of this imminent campaign was enough to help defeat the measure on the Assembly floor, in a vote of 42 to 20. This victory was achieved at minimum cost—with some creative copy writing and about $10 in postage.

ADVOCACY IN ACTION: An Ad Linked to Action

In The California Wellness Foundation's "Campaign to Prevent Handgun Violence Against Kids," paid TV spots encouraged the target audience to call a toll-free number to receive a citizen participation kit. This kit included postcards that could be sent to elected officials asking them to support policies to prevent handgun violence. Because the advertisements were placed in time slots when high numbers of supporters of the campaign message were known to be watching, the message found a receptive audience, and large numbers requested the kits and followed up with the requested action of communicating with opinion leaders.

At the same time, a database of about 10,000 opinion leaders (e.g., elected officials, school principals) from around the state received mailings of resource kits linked to the message of the commercials. These kits, titled "First Aid for What's Killing Our Kids," included fact sheets, policy papers, hard copy of the ads, public opinion poll data, and related materials. The paid media campaign, because it focused primarily on the large number of handguns, was quite controversial and thus generated news coverage as well—another form of communication to opinion leaders. In this way, the groundwork was laid for further action that would advance the policy agenda.

All Talk, All the Time: Radio Opportunities

Talk radio can be a useful resource for getting your views out to the community and building support for your position. The advantages of talk radio include a potentially large audience, no cost (except for preparation time and pursuing a booking), extensive airtime, and an opportunity to use notes. Calling in to a radio talk show can also be a good chance to practice making your points with relatively little risk. The downside of talk radio is that you can get abused badly by a host who doesn't agree with you; suffer through a half hour of news, traffic, weather, and commercials before you get to speak; and end up getting framed rather than doing the framing.

Before you decide to go on a talk radio show consider the following:

- What will be the position of the host? Have you heard him/her talk on the issue before?
- What is the style of the host? Does the host strive to create conflict and controversy?
- Will someone else be on with you either in the studio or via remote setup? What can you find out about this person?
- How does your talk radio appearance advance the policy issue with which you are concerned?
- Do the show's producers have telephone call-ins? Is it aired at a time when you are sure you can get at least a few friends or colleagues to call in with supportive questions?
- What will the show do if you turn them down? If the answer is that they'll find another speaker whom you don't think knows the issue as well as you, then maybe it's worth your time to do the show. On the other hand, if it is a hostile show and without your participation, the producers might just drop the topic entirely, then it may be strategically wise to turn it down.

Getting on the Air as a Caller

In large media markets, it can be a challenge to get onto a talk radio show as a caller because so many people call in to the show. Usually, a producer screens the incoming calls and decides who should be put through to the host, so it's important to be ready with your perspective in a nutshell. Think of this as another kind of pitch. A few pointers for getting on the air:

- Be passionate about what you believe in and how it relates to you personally.
- Try to call into shows with which you are familiar. If you don't know the host's perspective, you can be sideswiped by tactics or tones that you haven't anticipated.
- Be tenacious. If you disagree with the perspective of the host or the guest, be sure to tell this to the producer; your call may get priority because conflict and disagreement are interesting.
- Be comfortable. It may help you to jot down a few notes about what you want to say, but don't read your comments from a script. Remember that no one knows who you are, and this is a good chance to practice talking about your issue.
- Don't call from a speakerphone. If you're on a car phone, let the producer know; he or she may put you on the air sooner.

- Be sure to turn your radio all the way down before calling. The seven-second delay used by most radio stations will throw off your concentration if you can hear the program in the background.

Cast a Net: Advocacy Online

The Internet provides a valuable communication resource for advocates. In a way, trying to explain how to use this vast, information-rich technology is much like talking about how to use a library and thus far beyond the scope of this book. However, we thought it would be useful to provide some tips to help you organize a net strategy.

Think about how the Internet can support your overall policy and advocacy goals. Always have a specific purpose in mind when you "surf the web." In this way, it will become more manageable because you will go into it with a purpose rather than to wander—you can save a lot of time.

There are several reasons why you might want to use the Internet:

Check out what the opposition is up to and learn more about how they talk about the issue. Go to the web page of groups who oppose your issue, and get some insight into their language and strategies.

For example, an advocate for gun safety policies might check out the National Rifle Association's home page at http://www.nra.org to see what the opposition is up to.

Get data to help you build your information packets and support your arguments. State and federal governments provide web sites where you can access the latest data on health and social issues. Often, these sites have copies of daily news releases summarizing government reports.

The same gun control advocate can find information on gun injuries from the U.S. Department of Health and Human Services' National Center for Health Statistics web site, at http://www.cdc.gov/ncipc/osp/usmort.htm

Get ideas for policy and strategy from groups working on the same issue. Although your organization may not have a web page, other groups working on the same issue might. Nonprofits typically have basic information about issues such as fact sheets, background briefs, names of key legislators, and so on.

For action updates and the latest information on gun policy issues, gun control advocates might check the Pacific Center for Violence Prevention's website at http://www.pcvp.org (see Figure 8.2) or the National Center to Prevent Handgun Violence's site, http://www.handguncontrol.org/

Figure 8.2. An Example of a Website's Home Page

Get specific, timely feedback on problems you are addressing. You can use e-mail to seek advice from advocates on your side via an e-mail listserv. You can pose a problem to dozens or even hundreds of people and get useful feedback. For example, a community group thinking about advancing an ordinance to limit billboard advertising might ask if there are any model ordinances available. This can save significant time and money.

Private invitation-only listservs are available for advocates on a wide range of issues. Ask your colleagues about e-mail lists you might join.

Check how your issue is being covered by searching newspapers online. Search for your topic, and get an idea of who is covering your issue and what is being said about it.

For example, search *USA Today* online at http://www.usatoday.com or entire databases of newspapers for a fee at http://www.lexis-nexis.com

Make it a habit to check home pages you're interested in on a weekly basis. Information can be updated frequently, and you should stay current.

Don't overlook the benefits of creating your own website to provide information on your organization and advocacy activities to your colleagues. Just bear in mind that unless you establish a password-protected site, anyone can access the information on your page; be careful about revealing sensitive advocacy strategies or media plans in such a public forum.

Summary

Our ninth rule is: **Consider all kinds of media in your strategy.** Paid advertising, talk radio, the Internet, and various forms of alternative media can be useful in supporting your overall strategy for change. Paid advertising can be a good investment of limited resources. It can increase the visibility and credibility of your issue, reinforce the efforts of other advocates in the field, generate news stories, and reach key decision makers in a timely way. Talk radio can be a useful resource for getting your views out to the community and building support for your issue. The Internet is an evolving medium with great potential. At the least, it offers a wealth of information and a means to communicate quickly with others in your field, even though they may be on the other side of the world. Alternative media include various weekly newspapers, local access television, non-English language media, and other ethnic media. All these are potential outlets that you can use to build support for your issue and reach key audiences.

Deciding which media outlets to approach will emerge from your overall strategy (Chapter 1); you may use different outlets as the policy environment changes. To be sure you are using the most powerful outlet for your objectives, among other measures of your effectiveness, you will want to evaluate your efforts. It is to the topic of evaluation that we now turn.

9

EVALUATING YOUR
MEDIA EFFORTS

"Would you tell me, please, which way I ought to go from here?"
"That depends a good deal on where you want to get to," said the
   Cat.
"I don't much care where—" said Alice.
"Then it doesn't matter which way you go," said the Cat
"—so long as I get *somewhere*," Alice added as an explanation.
"Oh, you're sure to do that," said the Cat, "if you only walk long
   enough."

Lewis Carroll, Alice in Wonderland

Strategic media work is part of a long term process to promote policy change. Such change is difficult, time-consuming, and complex. Feedback is critical to determine how you can improve your performance in the next encounter.

An evaluation answers questions about the work you did. When evaluations are designed well they can help you understand how you did this time and give you the information and insight you need to improve next time. When they are designed poorly, they are a waste of time. In this chapter, we offer a framework to help you evaluate your media advocacy effort. Our assumption is that most groups won't have the resources necessary to do large, complex evaluations and that, even if they did, determining the precise contribution media advocacy made to an overall policy advocacy effort would be enormously difficult. But even an organization on a shoestring budget needs to know whether it is achieving what it intended. In fact, especially when resources are limited, it is important to assess whether you are using them wisely. Evaluation can help you do just that.

Rule 10:
*Use evaluation to refine your media strategy
and improve your effectiveness.*

**Why Do an
Evaluation?**

We have a very pragmatic view of evaluation, based on Michael Quinn Patton's utilization-focused evaluation.[1] The idea is to design the evaluation around how it will be used. As we have said, you can't have a media strategy without an overall strategy—you must know what you want before you go asking for it. Similarly, Patton's idea is that you can't design an evaluation unless you know how it is going to be used. In general, he says, evaluations are used to either make judgments, facilitate improvements, or generate knowledge. Different audiences might have different uses for evaluation:

• **Funders** might want to know why they should support media advocacy. More than once, funders have asked us, "How do we know whether media advocacy is a worthwhile investment?" An evaluation focused on results would help funders answer that question; the primary users of the evaluation would be foundation program officers, Boards of Directors, or those who make grants in city and state government.

• **Advocates** might want to know how to make their media efforts more effective. They would want to know whether their activities were implemented as planned, and whether their actions had the intended outcome. The primary users in this case would be the media advocates themselves.

• **Academics** and others not directly involved in the activities might want to understand media advocacy in a larger context and generate knowledge for others. The primary users would be those who want to learn from others' experience with media advocacy.

Patton suggests that once you have determined whom the evaluation is for, you can then figure out which are the best questions to ask to explore what you want to know, figure out how to get the information to answer those questions, and then provide that information to the people who want it in a way they can use it. In this chapter, we focus on designing an evaluation that will be useful to the media advocates themselves. Consider these ideas simply a starting point, for if an evaluation is going to be useful, those who are going to use it should be involved in shaping it from the start.

The Real Story: Case Studies as Evaluation Tools

Most evaluations of media advocacy have been case studies: the story of what happened and why in a specific media advocacy effort.[2] Most case studies were done to distill lessons so other media advocates could learn from past mistakes and success. Case studies can be useful ways to gather information about media advocacy from different points of view—the advocates, their opponents, the targets of the media advocacy, and the journalists who covered the story could each add insight into what happened and why.

Case studies[3] have described media advocacy efforts in the areas of alcohol, tobacco, public housing, HIV/AIDS, and violence prevention. One lesson from these stories is that each media advocacy effort is unique, and the outcomes will be influenced by local circumstances as well as the goals and objectives of the advocates. But there are also similarities across media advocacy efforts. David Jernigan and Patricia Wright distilled lessons from 15 case studies in the areas of alcohol and tobacco that can help guide advocates when they shape campaigns, choose spokespeople, relate to members of the media, handle confrontation and controversy, and find and use resources.[4] We have learned a lot from these case studies on media advocacy, and applied many of their lessons throughout this book.

Designing an Evaluation: Which Questions Should You Ask?

Your media work is done strategically, and your evaluation should be strategic as well. A good evaluation design can help you observe what is going on, react to it, and, if necessary, adapt what you are doing based on your observations and assessments. The best evaluation is a living work in progress to assist you in carrying out your goals and objectives effectively, not a report that collects dust on a shelf, completed long after the work is done.

Patton's questions can guide your evaluation planning:

- What do you want to know?
- Is that information available?
- How will you get that information?
- How will it be used?

With these questions, you can design a useful evaluation that will become a tool to help you improve the work.

What do you want to know?

Ask yourself what you want to know about the media advocacy you and your group are doing. You may want to find out information about your personal effectiveness and growth interacting with journalists, your organization's process of planning and implementing media advocacy, or how others react to the coverage your issue receives. Consider the following questions that might guide a media advocacy evaluation.

- **How did you do?** News time is not like real time; an interview with a journalist, especially a live interview, can go by so quickly it seems like a blur and you can't remember what you said. Or worse, you remember what you meant to say but left out. On a personal level, an evaluation can help you assess your own interactions with journalists.

- **Did you do what you intended?** This question might also be simply, what happened? You then compare what happened with what you had planned. This question can help you assess the process of doing media advocacy, from planning a media event to pitching stories and responding to journalists' questions. For example, if you planned to hold a morning news conference and then be available to follow up with journalists in the afternoon, you might want to review how the process went. Was your timing right? Were journalists able to reach you in the afternoon?

- **Was your issue covered by the news media that your target sees or reads?** Where did the coverage appear? Is it where you wanted it to appear? What is good about that outlet, for your purposes? Where else might you want the coverage to appear?

- **Was your story told in the way you had hoped? Did your frame define the coverage?** This is usually a key question for advocates. Most of the issues advocates work on are important to the public's health and safety and society's well-being, and so they get the attention of journalists. But the solutions to the problems are generally heavily contested (if they weren't, there would be no need to use media advocacy). Therefore, assessing whether the issue got treated from a policy perspective and included the solution for which you are advocating is usually very important.

- **Have you become a source for the journalist?** Social change takes time and is often incremental. This means that media advocacy efforts usually involve a series of encounters with journalists over extended periods of time. If you are building relationships, you and your organization will become a source for journalists, which means that not only do you call them to alert them of good stories but that they call you when they have questions on your issue. An evaluation can help you determine whether this is happening.

- **Did your media work help you build community support for the overall program goal?** The process of creating and implementing good media plans—working with others to establish goals and objectives, framing the issue, creating news, or reacting to breaking news—is an opportunity to expand the network of support for an issue. A reasonable focus for the evaluation may not just involve media coverage but how the organization worked together with others to accomplish a goal.

The information you collect for the evaluation is dependent on your desired outcome for the target of your media advocacy. For example, your overall goal might be to pass an ordinance banning gun shows on county property. Your target is the county Board of Supervisors. Your media advocacy objective might be to have an article on the gun show issue appear in the local newspaper. Furthermore, you'd like that article to include quotations from your coalition members and others describing the problems the neighborhood is having because of the gun shows. And, you'd like the article to appear the day before the Supervisors' vote, so the community's concerns will be fresh in their minds. You can find out how you did from the news outlets where you pitched the story, by monitoring the media, and by talking with reporters, policymakers, and others.

**Gathering the
Information
to Answer
the Questions**

Monitor the media

Review the news and assess whether it is covering your issue adequately. Clip the articles from print sources or record the TV news when you know it will be covering a story you care about—then read, watch, and discuss the coverage. Pay attention to who reports on your issue and how they present it, so you can update your media list. Identify what's missing in the coverage, and practice articulating the frame. If you had been a journalist doing the story, what elements would you have included? Whom would you have interviewed? When you have analyzed the coverage, send materials to reporters to give them additional background and connect them to your group and your perspective. That is an immediate way evaluation can feed back information into your ongoing media advocacy project and to the journalists covering your issue.

Monitor yourself

If your evaluation questions revolve around your personal performance with journalists, you'll need to keep records of what you did. Tape your appearances on the news and review them with someone who can give you objective feedback. You can improve in the next interview and increase your confidence. Remember that you are an important variable in the story and that you have made a contribution, even if you didn't say everything you had hoped to say. This tape will prove very useful in improving your interactions with journalists.

Usually encounters with reporters are one-on-one, so if you can share some of that experience with others, you'll be able to enhance your own abilities, as well as let your colleagues learn from your work. For example, during a telephone interview with a journalist, we'll jot down the questions we're being asked. Afterward, we try those questions on each other, comparing others' answers with what we said. The process helps us think about how to improve our responses the next time and gives our colleagues a chance to practice answering actual questions from a reporter.

Interview key parties

Ask those who know. If you are curious about why a story is not interesting to the local reporters, ask them. If you want to know about policymakers' reaction to a news story, ask them. In our case study of how the Oakland, California, Coalition on Alcohol Outlet Issues used media advocacy to reduce the number of alcohol outlets in that city, we asked city council members' staff how they reacted to the news the coalition had generated. They said that the coverage was an important way the policymakers learned about the issue and their constituency's support for the issue.[5]

Integrate Feedback: Use the Evaluation Process to Improve the Work

Discuss your media advocacy efforts with your colleagues, friends, and critics. Media advocacy evaluation might be as simple as 20 minutes set aside at a monthly coalition meeting to discuss what the group has done, whether it went the way it was planned, what the response was, and how everyone thinks it might be improved next time. Or the time might be used to discuss recent news coverage or a media advocate's encounter with a journalist. The point is to reflect on what you are doing and share those reflections with your colleagues.

ADVOCACY IN ACTION: Assessing Media Efforts

People Reaching Out (PRO), a violence prevention coalition in Riverside, California, assessed its media advocacy efforts by examining its news releases and asking:

Which ones got a good response? Why?
Which news releases didn't generate any calls? Why?
Was there too much information? Did the news releases include everything they should have?

Discussing these simple questions among themselves, PRO members learned that when they were concise and gave a contact name and number, their local newspaper, the *Riverside Press Enterprise,* responded by calling for more information. They realized that when they described the program in detail with longer news releases, they wouldn't get a response. They also realized that sometimes, they had neglected to include a contact's name. This assessment helped them improve their news releases, increase the calls they got from the *Press Enterprise,* and even increase their confidence in pitching follow-up stories.

Use the evaluation to enhance your group's shared understanding of media advocacy. For example, framing is a difficult concept to perfect—it is always evolving and improving as you try to better articulate metaphors and examples, adapt to changing circumstances, and counter your opposition. Your evaluation can be a useful tool to reflect on your group's ability to frame the issue effectively. Discuss articles together, ask each other about meaning, generate discussion about metaphor. Is the policy in focus? Using evaluation this way can enhance your ability to speak in multiple yet harmonious voices on the issue. Discussions can refine and deepen what you have to say. Feedback from others can improve it. Your evaluation can be the time your group sets aside to regularly examine framing issues together and to clearly communicate with one another about them.

Re-Dedicate Your Effort Based on New Understanding

The goal of evaluation described here has been improving the work, rather than simply judging the work. Evaluation doesn't have to be formal. It can be a simple reflection on what you've been doing—a time to be thoughtful about whether your media actions are being carried out in the best possible way and to consider improvements.

Careful reflection about your group's work together can do more than tell you about the media work you've done. It can enhance communication and understanding between group members, clarify your overall goals and objectives, support participant engagement and ownership of the media advocacy plan, and lead to improvements in your program's organizational development. By incorporating routine discussions about your media practices, the process of discussing and questioning those actions with each other will provide the learning necessary to improve the media advocacy work the group does together.[6]

Summary

Our tenth rule is: Use evaluation to refine your media strategy and improve your effectiveness. Evaluation provides feedback to keep you on track. It is critical to review what you do and make appropriate changes in your strategy. Evaluations should be designed based on what you need to know to increase your effectiveness. You can do this by posing relatively simple questions and setting time aside to review these questions with others and reflect on ways to increase your effectiveness. Evaluation doesn't need to cost a lot of money to be useful, but it will take some time. This time, however, can save a lot more time in the future and increase the likelihood that you will reach your ultimate goals.

In the end, evaluation can be as simple as asking, "How are we doing and can we do better?" It can be as important as shaping successful strategies to help you create social change.

Notes

1. This chapter draws from Patton, M. Q. (1997). *Utilization-focused evaluation* (The New Century Text, Edition 3). Thousand Oaks, CA: Sage. Please see that book for an excellent, comprehensive discussion of program evaluation.

2. See The Advocacy Institute. (1992). *Telling your story: A guide to preparing advocacy case studies.* Washington, DC: Author.

3. The case studies are presented in the following works, listed alphabetically.

Dorfman, L. (1989). *Using the media to prevent alcohol promotion to youth: A case study.* Prepared for the Office of Substance Abuse Prevention, Alcohol, Drug Abuse, and Mental Health Administration.

Gerber, L. (1995, February). *Henry Horner Mothers Guild: Tenants go public on public housing.* Bethesda, MD: University Research Corp.

Jernigan, D., & Wright, P. (Eds.). (1994). *Making news, changing policy: Case studies of media advocacy on alcohol and tobacco issues.* Washington, DC: Center for Substance Abuse Prevention, U.S. Department of Health & Human Services.

Seevak, A. (1994). *Tapping the hearts and thinking of everyday people: The city wide liquor coalition's fight to ban tobacco and alcohol billboards in Baltimore.* San Rafael, CA: The Marin Institute for the Prevention of Alcohol and Other Drug Problems.

Wallack L. (1994). Media advocacy: A strategy for empowering people and communities. *Journal of Public Health Policy, 15*(4): 420-436.

Wallack, L., Dorfman, L., Jernigan, D., & Themba, M. (1993). *Media advocacy and public health: Power for prevention.* Newbury Park, CA: Sage.

Wallack, L., & Sciandra, R. (1990-1991). Media advocacy and public education in the community trial to reduce heavy smoking. *International Quarterly of Community Health Education, 11,* 205-222.

Woodruff, K. (1996, August). Alcohol advertising and violence against women: A media advocacy case study. *Health Education Quarterly, 23*(3), 330-345.

4. Jernigan, D. H., & Wright, P. A. (1996). Media advocacy: Lessons from community experiences. *Journal of Public Health Policy, 17*(3), 306-330.

5. Seevak, A. (1997). *"Oakland shows the way": The Coalition on Alcohol Outlet Issues and media advocacy as a tool for policy change* (Issue 3). Berkeley, CA: Berkeley Media Studies Group.

6. Patton, 1997, p. 99.

10

CONCLUSION

---◆---

There are two foundation pillars of media advocacy: deep understanding of what moves the media, and realistic hopefulness.

Michael Pertschuk, Advocacy Institute

---◆---

In social change efforts, the stakes seem to get higher every year for advocates across the country. There is some success but never enough of it. Our hope is that the principles in this book can help make success more common. And you can start right now. Make a commitment to find an article on your topic and write a letter to the editor. While you are at it, write a letter to the reporter (if you don't know him or her) introducing yourself and include some background materials. Start thinking now about upcoming events that might be good pegs for pitching a story. Also, watch your local news tonight—switch around the channels—and write down the names of reporters who are doing stories related to your topic. Write down a few visuals that might be useful in illustrating the stories you want to see covered.

We urge you to bear in mind the 10 basic rules of strategic news media work when developing your strategy or helping other groups and organizations with their media efforts.

1. **You can't have a media strategy without an overall strategy.** Think of media in support of and in addition to other approaches, rather than instead of or in isolation from them.

2. **If you want to be taken seriously as a credible source for reporters, you need to take the media seriously.** You must pay attention to whether and how your issue is covered, so you can be more effective in your own media efforts. If you want to work effectively through the media, you need to *know* the media.

3. **Understand the conventions and values that drive journalists.** Journalists are professionals—learn how they go about their business and use the common ground you share to give them good newsworthy stories and advance your issues.

4. **Pitch stories, not issues.** Most advocacy issues have been around for a long time, and you need to look for new ways to make them interesting to journalists and news consumers. Journalists think in terms of stories. Issues can be vague and bloodless; advocates need to make issues come alive by crafting stories.

5. **Supply journalists with creative story elements that illustrate the solution you support.** These include good visuals, social math, media bites, and "authentic voices" who can tell compelling personal stories. These elements will help you focus on your solution: Remember that the problem may be easier to talk about than the solution, but the solution is more important.

6. **Make your news events count.** Plan carefully. Make sure that speakers, materials, and the setting all reinforce your key message. Know what you want to say, say it, repeat it in different ways, and have others say it.

7. **An interview is not a conversation.** Think of interviews as potential vehicles to get your message out. Stick to *your* agenda, not the reporter's. Don't get lulled into casual talking. Be purposeful and make your point.

8. **Use the opinion pages to reach policymakers and opinion leaders.** An editorial page strategy should be part of your media efforts, and it can be more effective than some news events in reaching the people who can make a difference on your issue.

9. **Consider all kinds of media in your strategy.** Radio, paid advertising, and alternative media outlets all have various uses and can be effective in advancing your goals. Be sure you know why a particular media outlet or approach is right for you now. Whatever media you choose, reuse the news: send copies of articles, op-ed pieces, and letters to supporters and policymakers.

10. **Use evaluation to refine your media strategy and improve your effectiveness.** Despite your best planning and most rigorous efforts, some things will sometimes just not work. Reconsider your strategies, take setbacks as a challenge, and most of all, don't give up on the importance of incorporating the news media as part of your strategy.

Finally, keep the larger picture in view. The goal is to create a fairer, more just society. The distribution of resources that results in some people having disproportionately more opportunity and resources than others is a fundamental issue of justice. Dan Beauchamp notes that, "Under social justice all persons are entitled equally to key ends such as health protection or minimum standards of income."[1] People's sense of social justice is played out in the kinds of policies that advocates advance: policies that try to redress the power imbalance by providing communities with increased capacity to influence the policy environment. Issues such as alcohol availability, handgun control, tobacco, and child care, to name a few, inevitably come down to what people see as fair and just rules for society.

As Vietnamese monk Thich Nhat Hanh explains,

> The problem is whether we are determined to go in the direction of compassion or not. . . . If I lose my direction, I have to look for the north star and I will go to the north. That does not mean I expect to arrive at the north star. I just want to go in that direction.

Applying the value of compassion to social problems means that your policies will emphasize prevention rather than punishment, equal opportunity rather than enhanced access for the privileged, social accountability rather than victim blaming, and mutual support rather than rugged individualism. The issues advocates struggle with are deeply entrenched and may not be resolved in your life time. Your *goal* may be to reach the North Star, but your *mission* is to better mark the path so that others can more clearly follow the direction with fewer obstacles. We hope that this book will help leave a trail that is more clearly marked and easier to follow.

Final Thoughts

Note

1. Beauchamp, D. (1976). Public health as social justice. *Inquiry, 12,* 3-14.

APPENDIX
Further Resources

Publications on Community Organizing and Advocacy

Reclaiming America: Nike, Clean Air, and the New National Activism, by Randy Shaw; University of California Press, 1999.

Community Organizing and Community Building for Health, edited by Meredith Minkler; Rutgers University Press, 1997.

Organizing for Social Change: A Manual for Activists in the 1990s, by Kim Bobo, Jackie Kendall, and Steve Max; Seven Locks Press, 1996.

The Activist's Handbook: A Primer for the 1990s and Beyond, by Randy Shaw; University of California Press, 1996.

Roots to Power: A Manual for Grassroots Organizing, by Lee Staples; Praeger Press, 1984.

Publications on Nonprofit Lobbying

Nonprofit Lobbying Guide: Advocating Your Cause and Getting Results, 2nd ed., by Bob Smucker; Independent Sector, Washington, DC, 1999.

"Lobbying rules create opportunity for charities," *Nonprofit Issues Newsletter*, October, 1998; published by Nonprofit Issues, Inc., Dresher PA.

Charity Lobbying and the Public Interest; Pamphlet published by Independent Sector, Washington DC, 1994.

Publications on Media

Making the News: A Guide for Nonprofits and Activists, by Jason Salzman; Westview Press, 1998.

We the Media: A Citizen's Guide to Fighting for Media Democracy, edited by Don Hazen and Julie Winokur; The New Press, 1997.

"Media Advocacy: A Strategy for Advancing Policy and Promoting Health," by Lawrence Wallack and Lori Dorfman; *Health Education Quarterly, 23*(3), 1996.

"Media Advocacy: Lessons from Community Experiences," by David Jernigan and Patricia Wright; *Journal of Public Health Policy, 17*(3), 1996.

Let the World Know: Make Your Cause News, by Jason Salzman; Rocky Mountain Media Watch, 1995.

Toxic Sludge Is Good for You: Lies, Damn Lies, and the Public Relations Industry, by John C. Stauber and Sheldon Rampton; Common Courage Press, Monroe, ME, 1995.

The Fight for Public Health: Principles and Practice of Media Advocacy, by Simon Chapman and Deborah Lupton; BMJ Publishing Group, London, 1994.

Media Advocacy and Public Health: Power for Prevention, by Lawrence Wallack, Lori Dorfman, David Jernigan, and Makani Themba; Sage Publications, Newbury Park, CA, 1993.

Making News: How to Get News Coverage for Disability Rights Issues, by Tari Susan Hartman and Mary Johnson; The Avocado Press, 1993.

The Why, Who, and How of the Editorial Page, 2nd ed., by Kenneth Rystrom; Strata Publishing Co, State College, PA, 1993.

Telling Your Story: A Guide to Preparing Advocacy Case Studies, The Advocacy Institute, Washington, DC, 1992.

Media Advocacy: Reframing Public Debate, by Michael Pertschuk and Phillip Wilbur; The Benton Foundation's Strategic Communications for Nonprofit Series, Washington, DC, 1991.

Prime Time Activism: Media Strategies for Grassroots Organizing, by Charlotte Ryan; South End Press, Boston, MA, 1991.

Media How-To Guidebook, by Media Alliance, San Francisco, CA, 1991.

Sources for Media Lists

Public Relations Plus, Inc. (1-800-999-8448): provides a directory of California news sources and one of New York for $149 each, including one 6-month update. Also available on diskette for about $350.

Bacon's Directory (1-800-621-0561): provides a national directory on Newspaper & Magazines and one on radio and TV; each is about $270, including one 6-month update. Also available on CD-ROM for about $995.

INDEX

About the Authors

Lawrence Wallack, DrPH, is Professor of Public Health at the University of California, Berkeley, and Director of the School of Community Health, College of Urban and Public Affairs at Portland State University. He was the founding director of the Berkeley Media Studies Group, an organization conducting research and training in the use of media to promote healthy public policies. He is one of the primary architects of media advocacy an innovative approach to working with mass media to advance public health. He has published extensively and lectures frequently on the news media and public health policy issues. He is the principal author of *Media Advocacy and Public Health: Power for Prevention* (Sage Publications, 1993). He is also co-editor (with Charles Atkin) of *Mass Media and Public Health: Complexities and Conflicts* (Sage, 1990). Dr. Wallack has appeared on *Nightline, Good Morning America,* the*CBS Evening News,* the *Today Show, CNN, The Oprah Winfrey Show,* and numerous local news and public affairs programs to discuss his research and to comment on policy issues regarding public health problems.

Katie Woodruff, MPH, is Program Director at the Berkeley Media Studies Group, which studies the process of news gathering and analyzes media content to support media advocacy training for community and public health leadership groups. Her research and training activities are directed toward groups interested in social change. She provides strategic consultation and media advocacy training to community groups working on a range of public health and public interest issues, including violence prevention, alcohol control, tobacco control, injury control, children's health, child care, and affirmative action. She also conducts research on news content and has published case studies and articles on applying media advocacy to public health and social justice issues.

Lori Dorfman, DrPH, is Director of the Berkeley Media Studies Group. Her current research examines how local television news and newspapers portray youth and violence. She edited *Reporting on Violence*, a handbook for journalists illustrating how to include a public health perspective in news coverage of violence. She has published articles on public health and mass communication issues and is a coauthor of *Public Health and Media Advocacy: Power for Prevention* (Sage Publications, 1993). She has served as a consultant for government agencies and community programs across the United States and Canada, working on a variety of issues including violence prevention, alcohol control, tobacco control, nutrition and exercise, injury control, child care, and childhood lead poisoning.

Iris Diaz is the Training Coordinator for the Berkeley Media Studies Group, where she designs and conducts media advocacy training for community groups and young people across the country. She has presented to national conferences and has extensive experience consulting with communities to understand and effectively use the power of the news media to promote policies that advance social and public health goals. Previously, she worked as an AIDS Counselor for the Shanti Project in San Francisco. She also has 10 years of television experience as Associate Producer and Producer of segments for children's programming, documentaries, specials, and health-care related videos at KRON-TV, KPIX-TV, and Kaiser Permanente in San Francisco.